More praise for

Legacy of the Blue Heron

"This book is essential reading for all who work with individuals who have learning disabilities and with their families....Harry Sylvester's message to those who counsel is powerful: One must connect through understanding and compassion in order to open the door for education and guidance. His message to parents is equally powerful: Understand, accept, offer love, be there, never give up, and seek the necessary help."

Larry B. Silver, M.D.,
Clinical Professor of Psychiatry at Georgetown University,
author of The MisUnderstood Child, *and a former president*
of the Learning Disabilities Association of America

"Harry Sylvester's tireless, devoted efforts on behalf of the Learning Disabled are legendary. In his book, he goes beyond merely defining the problem; he also offers pragmatic academic, social, and legislative solutions. His story — and the stories of his friends who have walked a similar road — are both informative and inspirational. The current professional literature is filled with tales of `famous people' with Learning Disabilities. But no story is more moving, meaningful, or motivational than the story of my good friend from the state of Maine. Read this book. Then read it again. Then pass it on to another."

Rick Lavoie, M.A., M.Ed., nationally known lecturer, author,
and consultant on learning disabilities, and former
president of the Riverview School on Cape Cod

Legacy of the Blue Heron

Living with Learning Disabilities

Harry Sylvester

former president,
Learning Disabilities Association of America

Oxton House Publishers
Farmington, Maine

Oxton House Publishers, LLC
P. O. Box 209
Farmington, Maine 04938

phone: 1-800-539-7323
fax: 1-207-779-0623
www.oxtonhouse.com

Printed in the United States of America

09 08 07 06 05 04 03 02   10 9 8 7 6 5 4 3 2 1

Publisher's Cataloging-in-Publication
(*Provided by Quality Books, Inc.*)

Sylvester, Harry (Harrison C.)
   Legacy of the blue heron : living with learning
disabilities / Harry Sylvester. -- 1st ed.
   p. cm.
   ISBN 1-881929-20-5

   1. Sylvester, Harry (Harrison C.) 2. Learning
disabled--United States--Biography. 3. Learning
disabilities. I. Title.

LC4818.5.S95 2002   371.9'092
                               QBI33-483

Cover design by Laurie Chapman of Washington, Maine. Stratton School photo on cover courtesy of Tom MacDonald of Eustis, Maine.

$\mathcal{T}$o my wife, Janet, who has become my partner in the learning disabilities work. Without Janet's interest and support, I would never have come to the point where I would write a book on learning disabilities.

and

To literally hundreds of people with learning disabilities who have shared their stories with me.

Foreword

This is a remarkable book by a remarkable man. Harry Sylvester started life as a youngster with serious learning disabilities. Now retired, he has been a successful mechanical engineer, business owner, and boatbuilder — and he still has the same disabilities with which he began the first grade in northern Maine. His book is first of all a story of persistence in the face of misunderstanding, a story of survival by patient perseverance through years of puzzlement and frustration. But it is much more. Harry Sylvester shares with us many lessons about learning disabilities, lessons that he learned the hard way, during the many years in which our larger society was itself just discovering what learning disabilities are. In so doing, he offers to spare us some of the deep individual and social pain that misunderstanding inflicts, if only we will truly hear his story. With uncommon common sense, he lays out coping tactics for the estimated 10% of us who have learning disabilities and describes productive strategies for the various social agencies that interact with them.

This book is a "must read" for teachers, school administrators, school board members, law enforcement officers, corrections officials, judges, and social service workers of all sorts. It is also a "must read" for some who have the most trouble reading — those who, like Harry Sylvester, have dyslexia or related learning disabilities. To make his words easier to read, Harry has asked that this book be set in a sans serif type style with extra space between letters and between lines. We at Oxton House are happy to comply with his wishes.

As Harry himself tells you in the Preface, he is a non-writer. This book was dictated. This is Harry Sylvester having a long talk with you in his living room, or maybe in yours. The words come off the page just as he would say them to you. The style is informal and unvarnished, but it's clear, wise, and compelling. Listen to him: enjoy his stories, share his feelings, and learn his lessons.

Bill Berlinghoff, Managing Editor
Oxton House Publishers

Preface

When I decided that I would like to write a book about my experiences in learning disabilities, I was facing a very difficult task, because my disabilities are so severe that I am an absolute non-writer. For me to write a book, I would have to rely on compensatory strategies.

My compensatory strategy has been a woman named Mary Grow. I met Mary about 15 years ago. I had just designed and launched a new 22-foot Whitehall sailboat. She came as a newspaper reporter to do a story on my new boat for the local newspaper. It happened that the photographer was late, and while we were sitting waiting, I started telling Mary about my experiences and work with learning disabilities. She became very interested and ended up writing several articles on learning disabilities and has been interested in the work that I have been doing ever since. I have dictated the material, and Mary has come once a week for a little over a year to transcribe the material onto my computer screen. With a lot of help from Mary, this material has been organized, edited and put into the form of a book. From the beginning, Mary has been careful not to change a single word without my approval. We have ended up thinking of this book as being in my voice.

Thank you, Mary.

When I was in my early 50s, I thought I was the only one in the world that had these strange problems with language – for me, particularly with reading, writing and spelling. I started hearing about learning disabilities and dyslexia and started a journey to find out what that all meant. I am very grateful to the many people who have given me insight into learning disabilities or supported me along the way, including:

Bob Abbott
David Anderman
Tony Bashir
Bob Broudo
Dale Brown
Lynn Cannon
Flora Champlin
Sheila Clark-Edmands
Bob Curry
Sue Ernst
Joan Esposito
Linda Felle
Phyllis Fischer
Mark Griffin
Hal Henderson
Rachel Henderson
Susan Jenkins
Jonathan Jones

Pat Kissire
Frank Klein
Ann Kornblatt
Rick Lavoie
Milele Lundrum
Leone Lunt
Hal McGrady
Melinda Parrill
Geoff Robbins
Arlyn Roffman
Sally Shaywitz
Larry Silver
Eileen Simpson
Jud Smith
Sally Smith
Sheldon Smith
Suzanne Stevens
Barbara Wilson

Of course, for better or worse, all the opinions expressed in this book are mine. In particular, none of them should be attributed to the Learning Disabilities Association of America or to any other organization I have been associated with. They are based on my personal experiences and reflect my personal feelings about how things are and how they ought to be.

X

Contents

✧✧✧✧✧✧✧✧✧✧✧✧✧✧✧✧

Introduction

    I come from a farm background, and when I was growing up spent a lot of time working outdoors and in the fields and just loved it. It also was a place where I could use my own abilities in the mechanical areas. Before I was 10 years old, I was driving trucks and tractors and operating all kinds of farm machinery better than any hired man. I could drive the tractor that hauled the mower, or the hay rake, or the potato digger, depending on the time of year. If I got going too fast and broke something, or if a gear broke or the potato digger got plugged up, I had the ability to fix it. I really looked forward to summers, to be out in the fields and away from school. I remember one spring, the last day of school was a school picnic, and I had the choice of going to the school picnic or driving a tractor all day. I drove the tractor.

    One year when I was 11 or 12 years old, we were haying, and it happened one day that my work was all caught up and I was just riding on a tractor with my father while he was raking. We were visiting and enjoying the time. All of a sudden in the field there appeared a blue heron. It was a young one, and it was learning to fly. It kind of bobbed around in the field, and would fly a little bit and then be on the ground, walking around. We watched the performance for a little while, until the blue heron drifted off the field into the edge of some bushes and trees.

    I got off the tractor and went exploring to see if I could find it. After a while, I spotted the heron in some brush near a rock pile. I picked up one of the rocks and threw it at the heron, and for some strange reason it hit the heron right in the head. Was I surprised, because one of the things that I can't do is throw anything! The heron was dead. It happens that in the part of the world that I grew up in, the blue heron was called a shit-poke, because it pokes around in the mud in the shallows of ponds and streams. So I hadn't really done anything wrong; what I had done was rid the world of one more shit-poke.

I started looking the bird over, and the first thing that struck me was, this bird is huge. Not only that, it seemed to be quite clean, and there was no bad smell to it. And it had some very interesting colors. I found the bird to be fascinating, and I carried it back to show my father. He thought I'd done a good job.

I became interested in the blue heron that day and started studying it. I was quite amazed at what I saw. I discovered that blue herons certainly do spend a lot of time in the shallow end of the lake, feeding and what looks like poking around in the mud. However, they're more apt to be feeding on small fish or frogs. They are huge and quietly go about their business. They are quiet and don't complain about anything, except once in a while if another blue heron encroaches on their territory, they might squawk about that. These huge birds can land in a tree, fold up their long legs, and roost for the night. They are beautiful, peaceful, intelligent and have lots to teach us. I feel very bad about the first one I encountered, but have had the opportunity to learn from them for many years.

When herons stand, they are very tall, and their long legs are very evident. This is just like me. They are huge, slow, and go about their business quietly without making lots of fuss. As I got into the learning disabilities field, I could see that the heron had a bad reputation, undeserved, just like me. The blue herons and I have quietly been trying to sneak through life without getting into trouble.

About 15 years ago, I started looking at learning disabilities, or dyslexia, for my own personal reasons. It was difficult to get information or find people who understood the questions that I was asking. However, I did manage to learn that I was not the only one in the world who had these strange language difficulties — in fact, I was very surprised to find that about 10% of the population have similar problems. I also learned that there was understanding and knowledge to help us figure out why our lives — in school, at work, and in our personal relationships — never seemed to work right. Soon I was answering questions that other people had about learning disabilities, and I quickly started using my experience and knowledge to help others. This was not a direction or field I had ever expected to go in; it just happened automatically, and it was a very natural direction to take.

This has been a spiritual experience for me. When I needed them, the right person has been there and the right opportunity came along. I haven't had to plan what I was going to do or how I was going to do it; it always seemed to work out the way it should be. All I had to do was not say "No" when someone asked me to do something in the field.

This direction has led me into many different roles, working with many different kinds of people. This book is an attempt to bring all of these experiences together, because they are all related. I hope that my readers will end up with a better understanding of what it means to have a learning disability, and that those with disabilities will find some solutions for their difficulties.

This book is personal, not technical. Some people argue, for example, over whether learning disabilities and dyslexia are different things; I don't care. From the beginning of my journey, I have been a member of the Learning Disabilities Association of America (LDA) and the International Dyslexia Association (IDA). In this book, I'm going to use the term "learning disabilities" (LD), because they're all related and I don't want to spend time working on definitions. My big interest is in doing something about them.

I find that in the field it is easy to talk about the academic issues — the difficulties in learning language and/or math.

Language disabilities and resulting poor communication not only lead to academic failure, they also lead to social failure. Both cause a loss of self-esteem and a lot of other social and emotional issues that don't tend to get dealt with in research, literature, or conversation. I find that these social/emotional issues sometimes can be more destructive than the academic issues, so I will try to emphasize them in the following chapters.

It is my hope that people reading this book will end up with a lot better understanding of learning disabilities. I use a lot of my own experience because this is the story that I know best. I talk about support group work in hopes that others will have the courage to get involved in this type of work. I try to be very open and honest about my experiences, in the hope that others will be able to share their experiences. It is through this kind of dialogue that we can get the world to understand about the struggle with language or mathematics.

What I hope to do is to educate people about the issues so that they can make changes, some of which are so dramatic that they can change people's whole lives. Sometimes this is a very easy task. For example, I was talking to a group of teachers taking a course in exceptionalities, for recertification. I was doing the LD piece. One of the things that I always talk about is the math disability. It happens that my disabilities are all in language, but many people struggle with math issues, especially advanced math. I don't spend a lot of time on math, but I never want to omit it. As I talked about math disabilities, a teacher in the back of the room asked a question or two. I started going into a little more detail, and suddenly she started to cry. When these things happen, I like to explore them and deal with them right on the spot. She explained that she and her husband were both engineers, and they had a daughter who was having math troubles in school. They couldn't understand why this was happening, because they were both so good at math and they couldn't understand how someone (especially someone in their family) could have a disability in advanced math. There had been lots of extra tutoring and time spent with the daughter, and it was pretty obvious that there had been a stress build-up in this family over the math difficulty. The woman kept sobbing and saying, "I want to get home so I can hug my daughter." This family will make a dramatic change over a five-minute conversation — so quick and so easy.

Other times, people get stuck and can't seem to move. We cannot make people change; we can only give them knowledge or information, and it is up to them to make the changes. For years now, I have been trying in many different ways to give people with learning disabilities the information and support they need to change their lives. This book is one more step in that direction.

How this book is organized

Legacy of the Blue Heron has two main sections. The first section (Chapters 1 – 5) describes the problems that learning disabilities can cause, both for the person who has the disability and for the whole society. This part is based largely on my personal experience, but I have included experiences shared with me by other people with learning disabilities. Many of these other people live in Maine, but I have worked with people all across the country.

The second section (Chapters 6 and 7) proposes solutions to the problems that learning disabilities cause. Again, these recommendations are based to a great extent on my personal experience. In running support groups, advising students and teachers in schools at all levels and holding office in local, state and national organizations, I have had many opportunities to find out what works and succeeds and what does not. Unlike when

I was in school and earning my living after school, today a lot of government and private money is invested in trying to help people with learning disabilities live happy and productive lives. It is important to spend the money on programs and techniques that achieve their goals, and not to waste it on methods that leave the victims of the experiment feeling even more like failures than they did before.

Three appendices provide definitions of some of the educational terms used in the book, a list of principal organizations dealing with learning disabilities, and a partial summary of the research on social costs associated with learning disabilities.

School Days

Learning disabilities didn't cause me any trouble in life until I walked into the first grade. It probably would have happened earlier, but when I started in there weren't any kindergartens. It was 1937, and I was five years old. The interesting thing about the date is that this was when Samuel Orton started writing his first papers on what was to be called dyslexia. It amazes me that so many people are still struggling with language and other related difficulties several generations later.

The Stratton, Maine, school in those days was a three-story wooden building, replacing one that burned not many years before I started, and quite modern for its time. The bottom level held the gym and the home economics room. From the entrance, a short flight of stairs led to the first floor where four classrooms, with two grades to a room, accommodated elementary-school students. The top floor was the high school. Each classroom had its own boys' and girls' bathrooms, each with a flush toilet and a little sink. The classrooms had lots of windows. The building had coal-fired steam heat, delivered to each room by a uni-vent, a cabinet with heating coils in it and a blower that circulated the air.

I think I was a lot like other kids in that I was nervous about going to school the first day. I was afraid I wouldn't find the right room and the right teacher. That part worked out well. The problem came within a few days, when I could not do my reading workbook. This book was set up so that you had to fill words in little boxes and connect up pictures with words. It all seemed like pretty simple tasks, but for me, it just simply didn't work. I think my teacher saw me as being bright enough, and if I would only try and pay attention I'd be able to do the work like the other students. Her first strategy was that if I stayed in at recess long enough, I would give in and do the workbook. The truth of the matter was, I would have done the workbook the very first day, if I could have. I stayed in for week after week — I don't really remember how long — and listened to the other kids playing at recess and having a wonderful time. I took my pencil and went back and forth on my reading workbook, and eventually I cut a slot right through the darned thing. I discovered when I held it up and fanned it in front of myself, I would get a nice white line suspended in space, and I thought this was really pretty special. When I demonstrated it to the teacher, she thought that that wasn't anything that anyone should do with a reading workbook.

When the time came that I did go out at recess, I thought that I would have the opportunity to play and run and have that good time. However, I discovered that nobody wanted to have anything to do with me, because there was something different about me. I feel that I not only failed to learn to read, I also failed recess.

The second strategy was that if I stood in the hallway at school long enough, then I'd learn to do my reading workbook. However, this didn't work either. The lonesome, boring hours I spent standing beside the classroom door separated me even more from the other students, and left me physically worn out. One day, I asked the teacher if I could have a chair to sit in, and the terse answer was No, I was to stand and I was to stand on that spot right there. As I look back, it's obvious I was being punished because the school didn't have an effective reading program for me. Luckily, I discovered that it was so quiet in the hallway that I could tell everything that was going on in the whole building. I did range around some, and spent time looking out a fire-escape window, which helped. I even thought about going down the short fire escape, running across the ball field into the woods and up Bigelow Mountain. The woods were not my scary place. School was the tough place.

I have only a few vague memories of the second, third, and fourth grades. I have worked on it, but think maybe I don't need to know what those years were like. In the third or fourth grade, whenever it is that we have to learn our multiplication tables, I was the last one in the class to be able to do a particular table — except, I do remember that when we were learning our nines tables, I could see how the nines tables work. Even though I was very young, I could see the system to figure out the answers; with a little practice I could make it work very quickly, and I was the first one in the class to be able to say my nines tables all the way through and have them right. My teacher asked me how I was doing that, and I tried to explain to her the system that I was using, but I couldn't seem to do it. She kept asking me about how I was doing it, and I couldn't seem to get her to understand. She ended up saying that the nines tables were the hardest ones to learn, and if I could learn the nines tables, I could have done all the others, if I had wanted to. So that was the end of my success in that story.

I do remember the fifth grade, explicitly, because that is the year that I failed. There was some brave talk that if I repeated the fifth grade, it would be work that I'd done once and would be easier the second time around, and that I would be a year older and more mature and that was going to help. However, the second year wasn't any better than the first year, and I didn't learn to read and write any more than I had before. All it did was add one more miserable year to my schooling.

I can remember that the teacher assigned us a story to write one day, and we were supposed to write the story and not worry about the spelling. For me, that was a wonderful experience, and I can remember being able to write my little story and it went off very quickly and easily and I even thought it was kind of fun. However, when she corrected the story, the only thing she did was correct the spelling. I told her that she had asked us not to worry about the spelling, just write the story, and that's what I had done, and it didn't seem right for her to correct the spelling; and I know that she didn't even read the story. So that was the end of my freedom to write, because I couldn't do the spelling part.

Another thing happened my first year in fifth grade, with the same teacher. I knew the teacher was mad at me lots of times because of the things I couldn't do. However, I also knew the difference between her being mad and her being disgusted. Sometimes when she would look at my papers as she was correcting them, I could tell by her attitude and motion and the way she snatched the paper that she was real disgusted with me, and I didn't really want to be so bad that people were disgusted with me.

The teacher I had for the second year in the fifth grade was a musician, and she brought her violin to school and played it for us. She taught us to read music — how to read the scales, and what the different notes meant — and for some reason, I understood how all of that worked and could easily write scales on music paper. I know now that music involves more logical skills than verbal skills, and musical learning takes place in a different part of your brain. Although I don't consider myself a musician, I do remember the music lessons as one of the few bright spots in fifth grade.

Even after my second year in fifth grade, things were no better for me in sixth or seventh or eighth grade. At a reunion recently, I met the teacher that I'd had in the seventh grade. I was very curious to know what she could remember about my success in school, and particularly my reading and writing. She had no recollection at all about any of that! However, she said right away that I was the class carpenter, and I didn't know what that meant. She said that she had a bunch of boys in that class that needed something extra in school, and the school allowed her to get some lumber and plywood and make some things during school, down in the basement. And I do remember that wonderful sheet of plywood. But she said she put me in charge, and that the whole process had worked very well, and the school was pleased with it, and it turned out to be a successful venture for some of us. One of the things I made was a set of bookends; my daughter has them now.

My first school success was when I arrived in high school and I got to Algebra I. This will sound funny to a lot of people, because that's the exact point where lots of people start having trouble. They've been very successful in school up to that point and can't do the advanced math. I could do the math! It took some time for me to realize that I could do it, I was so used to not being able to do anything in school. At first, I didn't pay attention and see what the algebra was all about, but after a little bit, I decided, Hey, I'm understanding this and I can do it, and my spelling's not holding me back. And I went on to become a top student in algebra, trigonometry, and geometry. I also could do and understand physics and chemistry. By this time, I was reading enough so that I could read a chemistry or physics assignment. I might have to do it several times, and it would probably be only a page or less, but I could handle the reading part, with extra time. However, my problems persisted in English. I couldn't write things and I couldn't spell and my reading wasn't very good. To do something like a book report was impossible.

I think my teachers in high school didn't know what to do with me, because I could do very well in some courses, but I just couldn't do the English. What happened was that I received grades on all of my non-English courses according to my success, and I always received a C in English, which was a gift. This led to what we now call "social promotion," and as I look back on my education, if I hadn't been socially promoted, my life wouldn't have turned out anywhere near as well as it has.

I did graduate from high school, on time, and supposedly was ready to move out into the world. I ended up being fifth in my class; this has always given me bragging rights. However, if anybody asked how many were in my high school graduating class, I was always in trouble; there were only five of us.

Because I graduated from a very small country school and had had so much difficulty in language, and I did want to go on to college, it was determined that I should go to prep school for a year. I had an uncle living in Worcester, Massachusetts, so I went to live with him and attended Worcester Academy as a day student for a postgraduate year. This was an eye-opener, for a country boy to be going to classes in a sport coat and tie, with a totally different class of student — more worldly, more sophisticated, richer, and the first foreign students I had ever met. It was a great experience, and I look back on it as being very worthwhile. I ended up on the varsity soccer team, even though I didn't know what soccer was when I enrolled (in 1950, almost nobody knew anything about soccer, and certainly not coaches at Stratton High School; it was a sport of the prep school circuit). Traveling with the team, I got to see other New England prep schools, and we won our share of games against them. Some of our foreign students had grown up with soccer and were really good players.

At Worcester I had some really fine teachers. I especially enjoyed my math and science teachers, Mr. Barthelman and Mr. O'Connell. But I soon discovered that I had taken all of my language difficulties with me. I eventually found myself in Dean Blossom's office, with my English teacher, who was saying that there was no way that he would pass me in English. The dean knew that I was doing well in other courses, and he was puzzled about the English. So he started asking me about this difficulty in a very nonthreatening way. I explained that my feeling was that I had somehow missed out on something back in the beginning, and that I needed to go back and start all over again. He thought that was a very interesting concept, but didn't see any reasonable way that it could be done. Now that I understand about these issues, what I was describing is what we call remediation, and I really did need to go back to the beginning and start with an entirely different kind of reading program, which is what we do every day now.

It happened that I was accepted at the University of Maine on my Stratton High School record. So I let the dean know that the next fall I was going to the University of Maine. It didn't

12

really make a lot of difference to me whether I graduated from Worcester Academy. But I did graduate with my class, and left one more English teacher in the dust. I am very grateful to Worcester Academy for that experience, even though I didn't receive any help with my language difficulties.

The next fall, I was off to the University of Maine, and, as you would expect, I again took all of my language difficulties with me. I had decided that I wanted to become a mechanical engineer, and this was the proper choice. I didn't have any trouble with mathematics again; as a matter of fact, I was helping tutor some of my classmates in algebra and trigonometry. Physics and chemistry were interesting and successful. But freshman English was the same old story. I started failing right away, and there were no social promotions. After failing English a couple of times, I took my grades in to my English teacher and asked what the story was, that I could do all the science, math, and technology but couldn't do the English. She looked at my grades, and, I think, was quite baffled by it, too, but had no idea what my difficulties were and just kind of shrugged me off. Later, she failed me, too.

The next year, I walked into my English class one morning to discover that the instructor had written part of my theme up on the board. All of the bad handwriting was mimicked, and the problems in spelling and grammar and everything that I have so much trouble with. I didn't have any idea what was going to happen, but after all of the students had gotten in and settled down in the seats, she announced to the whole class that she had received the worst paper she ever had gotten in her whole career. This person had no business being in college, and she couldn't understand how it had ever happened, and a real big mistake had been made and this person could never graduate from college. This went on for quite a few minutes; I don't really know how long, but I do know that I was so embarrassed and humiliated I sat there and pretended that it wasn't my work. I would have done anything to have been able to disappear out of the place.

The way it worked out at the university was that I got reacquainted with a delightful young lady named Janet, who could spell and read and do English. She had many other good qualities, too, and apparently she found some in me, because we were married between my sophomore and junior years.

Janet Mayo grew up in Wilton, Maine, went to Wilton grammar school and Wilton Academy, and was very successful in learning to read and write and spell and do those tasks. She was conscientious and hard-working, and it was very important to her to be a good student. Janet liked music, played the clarinet in the school band, and took piano lessons and learned to play the piano. Part of the time, her family lived on a farm, where she loved the animals. She had an older brother, and also was part of a larger extended family — many aunts and uncles and cousins for her to grow up with. Janet and I had met before she went to the university; we dated while she was a freshman and I a sophomore, and then we got married.

Janet helped me in my writing for English and technical reports; without this assistance I would never have been able to graduate. She could rewrite my themes for me and help me with all the work that I had to pass in. However, I couldn't take her to my English final exam. But between the two of us, I did finish my English requirements — with Ds, which gave me no grade points, but satisfied the requirement. (I accumulated enough hours in English to have a minor, though I never received it.)

As I have worked with people with learning disabilities over the past 15 years, almost everyone has told me the same story, in almost the same words. They could not read, write or spell; and their teachers told them if they cared, or worked harder, or paid attention, they would succeed.

In contrast to my struggles with English, my engineering courses were simple and easy and required very little study. I can remember my kinematics course (study of mechanical motion), which seems to be at the very center of my abilities and is a major course for mechanical engineers. I can remember preparing for the final exam. I had saved one whole evening to prepare. After about 20 minutes of study, I couldn't find anything that I needed to review. When the old professor turned back the final exams, he was a little bit excited. He said that there had been two real good finals; one of them was a 97, and the other one was a perfect exam, the only one that he'd ever had in his teaching career. And it was mine. Probably I hadn't even been challenged in that course. This instructor didn't even understand that he needed to alert me to my special ability in that particular area, and I never recognized it as being anything special; I just chalked up my perfect final to good luck.

I had another instructor, in machine shop, who seemed to understand how I should be educated. It happened that our machine shop had some old lathes that were line-shaft driven and all worn out. I was working on one of those lathes one day when the instructor came by to see how I was doing, and I made the comment that I wasn't quick enough to get one of the new, modern lathes. His reply was that anybody could do good work on those new lathes, but you had to be first-class to turn out good work on these old lathes. He gave me a little demonstration as to how the headstock was worn, and the tailstock was also out of line, and walked off and left me. He had challenged me to turn out good work on an old lathe, and I did.

It happened, in this class, that we had an upperclassman who had failed machine shop. I could hardly understand how anybody could do this, but I can remember seeing the instructor spending all kinds of time standing right at the elbow of that student, and explaining to him every step he needed to take. He was being very explicit with that student, and he had been very implicit with me. This instructor had a natural ability to teach. (The terms "explicit" and "implicit" will be discussed later.)

The interesting thing about this instructor was that he had very severe difficulties in calling the roll for attendance. In fact, the first time he called the roll, we couldn't figure out what names he was calling and we didn't know who should answer. Finally, one of the kids caught on and figured out who he was, and said, "Here." Some of the names were so mispronounced that we ended up calling each other by our new assigned names. For example, a kid named John York ended up being called John Yokie.

As I look back at going to the university, it occurs to me that I probably spent as much time on English as I did on all of my other courses combined. With all of that work and time and energy, I didn't make any gains in the English area, and I wasn't any better at it at the end of college than I was when I came in. So that was actually a real complete waste of time. And I wonder what would have happened if I had taken that amount of time and energy and put it toward doing the things that I could learn. I might have gone way beyond what I've been able to do, if I'd been able to enhance my abilities instead of spending all that time struggling with my disabilities.

I graduated, again on schedule, and was ready to move out into the world as an engineer — one who couldn't write and was reading at a very low level, but had exceptional talent in the mechanical area and didn't know it.

I tell this story about disabilities because it is the one that I know best, and I can go into a lot of detail about the things that happened along the way and help other people understand the difficulties. But as I look back, I can see that a lot of other people I went to school with had learning disabilities, too. Now that I know more about it, some of them have shared their stories with me, so I am discovering that I wasn't alone in my difficulties; many other people have had the same struggle that I have had. We were all so ashamed of our literacy problems that we didn't talk about them and didn't have a chance to compare notes and realize that we weren't alone. These stories that have been shared with me are very personal, and the people who have done this are not public figures, and I am reluctant to include a lot of these stories, because I wouldn't want to embarrass anybody. But their stories have a value that's hard to ignore, so I'm including pieces of them here and there, without mentioning names.

It takes a long time to realize that there isn't anything wrong with being learning disabled or dyslexic. It means that we have different abilities and disabilities than the norm. Some people are not musical, and it doesn't matter; they still succeed in school and in life. Other people are not athletic, and it doesn't matter. Unfortunately, in a society where language and math are so important, for those of us who cannot do language or math it does matter. Our differences become disabilities.

Back when I was in school, nobody understood about learning disabilities and problems with language and difficulties in learning. Today, things are much different. Most people have at least heard of learning disabilities or dyslexia. There have been lots of exciting changes in education, and I think this is a very exciting time to be working in the learning disabilities field, because we know now how to do so much more for students who have difficulties in school. The National Institutes of Health (NIH) and others have done a lot of research in the last few years, and they have come up with a lot better understanding of the process for learning language. It also validates some of the work that we had done in the past. Some of the ideas we had about reading were correct, but it also gives us new insights and new thinking to help with developing a lot more effective programming.

But we still do have lots of people walking around who were educated without benefit or knowledge about their abilities and disabilities. I didn't have any help; neither did my children in the 1960s; but my grandchildren received some help as they attended school in the 1980s and 1990s. We still have a long way to go to see that everybody who has a learning disability can live and work up to their potential and take their full place in society.

We now know that people like me who have a hard time learning to read and spell have what is called "poor phonemic awareness." This means that there is nothing wrong with our ears — we hear language, but we have real problems in learning to process it in a way that lets us learn how to read and spell.

We don't hear all of the little bits and pieces of sound that make up language, because our minds have trouble processing the sound. Some of us also have a hard time processing spoken language fast enough to keep up with conversations, especially when several people are talking. It is hard for me to explain it, because I have never listened to language with a mind that processes and handles language very easily. I have always had to struggle with language, in both oral and written form. I would just like to know what it is really like for language to work easily.

On the other hand, when it comes to a piece of machinery, I hear all of the little bits and pieces of sound within that machinery, such as vibrations or a bearing beginning to get worn, and I automatically know right away where the trouble is, what it is, and what needs to be done to correct it. It comes so quick and fast that I don't even need any processing time. For example, in the 1960s I was head engineer in a small metal finishing plant in Massachusetts. One morning as the plant was coming on line, people starting up machinery and moving around supplies, blowers coming on, I was walking down through the center aisle of the plant and I heard the faintest little "ting" in one of the big hundred-horsepower electric motors. I knew instantly that an oil ring in a bearing had swung and hit the inside of the casing. I also knew instantly that for that oil ring to have done that, it meant there was no oil in the bearing. When I got back to that electric motor, I discovered right away that the oil filler pipe had been broken off, accidentally, and lay in a puddle of oil on the floor under the bearing. Everything was shut down without damage. Even to this day, it seems like a miracle to me that I heard that little tiny sound above all the other sounds in the room, understood what it was, and discovered the problem before anything was damaged.

For myself, I know that it is very difficult for me to learn the language implicitly, just by being exposed to it, but I can learn a system to handle it. Learning a system requires processing, but it does work. It has to be taken further by repetition to develop the automaticity which gives us good fluency.

I think we all learn something by first having to do it as a cognitive process or a thinking process. For instance, when we first started to write, I can remember that we had a big fat pencil, and everybody struggled, and they had to concentrate to make it work. I can remember that most of my classmates quickly started writing easily and well. But I have never been able to write freely. In school, my papers were always a terrible mess; I was always making mistakes in words, and erasing out and putting words back in. Sometimes they'd go back with the same mistake they had the first time, and have to be erased again. Even though I became a real eraser expert, I still did not have a decent-looking paper to pass in. This whole thing has remained a cognitive process, or a thinking process. I still have to stop and think how the letters are written, what should be capitalized, and how the punctuation should go in. I know now that one of my language difficulties is called *dysgraphia*, which means the inability to write correctly and easily, and that my classmates had developed *automaticity,* the ability to write without thinking about each movement.

Also, I have extreme spelling problems; I have to try to figure out how words are spelled as I'm writing them. This is a cognitive process. I also struggle with knowing how to handle the grammar, which is a cognitive process for me. And I'm just like everybody else — I have to edit the material and get it ready to go down in written form. This is another cognitive process. I'm told that we can do only one cognitive process at a time, so it is no wonder that I am blocked when it comes to writing. Most people develop automaticity in the first three steps; the only thing they have to do is get the material ready to be written, and that's the only cognitive process that they deal with.

I see this process as being the same in all of our learning. We all start out very shaky on a bicycle, and have to think about which way to turn the front wheel so that it will keep us upright, and then after a while we do it automatically without thinking. (This explains why people can talk on a cell phone and eat a big Mac while they drive.)

Many of us who have language difficulties also have short-term memory problems, and the short-term memory problems make it even harder for us to handle language. I can't retain words or random numbers, and in school I couldn't do things like copy written material off the board. I would have to look up at a word several times to get it down on my paper; I could remember only two or three letters, then have to look up again, and repeat it until the word was done, and then go on to the next word. This was a lot of processing, and I never could get the materials done in time, and many times I made mistakes.

I needed explicit, direct instruction in language, which I never received; and consequently, I never developed the ability to handle language well. On the other hand, I have very strong natural abilities in the spatial area, the ability to see things as they are in your mind, like pictures. If you gave me instructions on how to get to your house in written form, it would be a real struggle for me. If you gave me a little map to show how to get to your house, I could take a quick look at the map, put it in my pocket and very soon arrive at your house. I can retain that picture of the map, but I can't retain the language.

This spatial ability also gives me good skills in building things and repairing things, because I can see the projects in my mind and retain all of the information very easily and accurately. This spatial ability gave me an interest in mechanics very early. I had a metal turning lathe when I was in junior high school, and by the time I got to high school I was starting to become a machinist. During high school I took an interest in mechanics, and by the time I graduated from high school I was rebuilding tractor and automobile engines. This was all self-taught, with a little advice from a mechanic. This is an example of very implicit education. I didn't even need a vocational school or formal instructors; all I needed was to have a project that I wanted to do and I found the tools to do it and the advice I needed, and I enjoyed every minute of it.

From the beginning of my school days, I was told directly, and also indirectly in many ways, that the reason that I didn't learn to read and write was because I didn't try, I didn't pay attention, I didn't want to, and it was always my fault. The truth of the matter was that I wanted to read very, very much. I had been read to, I knew what was in books, and I wanted to be able to get it out myself. I also wanted to please my teacher, like all the other kids did, and have her say something nice about me, too.

This was not isolated with just me; I find that this is a universal condition with all people that have learning disabilities. When I'm dealing with people, I very seldom use the word "all," but I do use it in this instance, because I can't remember anyone who has not had these kinds of difficulties; and they wanted to succeed just as much as I did. Many of us have even been punished because we didn't learn to read and write. That may not be happening as much now, but it has happened to many, many people in the older generations; we have been blamed for the failure which really wasn't our fault.

The other side of that is, those who are teaching school usually have pretty good language abilities; they have never experienced the difficulties those of us with language difficulties have, so they don't know what it's like to have to process language. They are also very organized, and have very little understanding of people who aren't. It's their job to turn out a bunch of good little readers with neat penmanship and good study habits, and when somebody like me comes along, it really messes up their whole life. They tend to be angry with those children who (as they see it) won't do work that is assigned, and to have very little patience with them. So between the two factions we have had lots of misunderstandings, and it has taken us a long time to get by all these troubles.

Many times, teachers' strategies to get the students to do the work they want them to do become punitive. I have asked other adults what happened to them in school, and what the teachers did. They have told me stories about things like they were put in a storeroom with a book and told not to come out until they could read; they were put in a cloakroom away from the rest of the class and told not to disturb anybody; or they were told to go down in the basement and spend their days with the janitor. Sometimes deals are struck when children get older, to the effect that, the teacher will say if you don't give me any trouble or cause any problems in the class, I'll give you a passing grade.

I have ended up with a lot of pretty negative thoughts about educators, particularly English teachers. I have met people that I thought were really fine people, and have been quite surprised to discover that they were English teachers. So, as I've worked in the field of education and learning disabilities, I have gotten to know a lot of educators at all levels, and I have had to change my thinking somewhat. I have done in-service programs for teachers on many, many occasions, and I am finding that there are a lot of wonderful, conscientious, hard-working people out there. They have to contend with their administrators, deal with parents, pay attention to laws, rules and regulations, do way too much paperwork and fit too many children into crowded rooms. On top of that, they have to find some time to educate our children, even when they may not have learned enough about learning disabilities to do that effectively for all of them.

Work Experience

After I graduated from college, my friend Keith Morrison and I started up an International truck dealership in Auburn, Maine. My skills were just right for doing this kind of work. We started the business from scratch, and one of the things that we had to do was put up a commercial steel building, which I did a lot of, with a high-school kid for a helper. We also had to buy trucks, stock parts, set up bookkeeping and record-keeping systems, hire office help, mechanics and a parts person, and do all the other jobs to get a business up and running. I was able to do my share even of the paperwork, and Keith and I got along surprisingly well. The first few years we worked long hours and it was challenging and exciting getting the business going. But after a few years, when the business was running, and I was spending most of my time with customers and delivering trucks, I thought more and more about doing something in the engineering field that I was really trained to do. After a while, I sold out my share of the business to my friend and partner. He still runs that business and uses many members of his own family to operate it. It has grown to the point where there are two dealerships, one in Auburn, Maine, and one in Portland, Maine. So the company still goes, and it's known as Morrison and Sylvester, Inc.

I went back to the University of Maine placement service and told them I was interested in an engineering job. They found me one at the Oxford Paper Company mill in Rumford, as a senior field engineer in the construction department. This was a pretty natural place for me to end up because I was a mechanical engineer and in the State of Maine there are a lot of jobs in paper mills for engineers. I was a straight mechanical engineer and hadn't had any pulp and paper training, so I didn't know anything about paper making or paper machines or any of the related equipment. But the first morning I walked into that paper mill, it was to me a place like heaven. Fantastic huge machines, and I was going to get to work on them and get to know them and I was even going to get paid for working there! A good spot.

I remember the first day (and this is the day that's always so hard on a new job, when you don't know anybody, and don't know the crews and don't know enough about anything to get anything done). My immediate supervisor, Oley Bangs, said that the construction department was rebuilding a paper machine. He took me up there to where the job was, and he said, "I want you to just study this machine all over, from one end to the other and down both sides."

He went off and left me there. I was just fascinated. I looked that machine all over to see how it was made and how it worked and all the details about it. I spent a long time going down the length of the machine and started up the back side, looking at the drives and figuring out how they all worked and how they all related to running the machine. I came across a crew of men working on a drive for the drier section. I watched them for a few minutes, and then I got up close enough so I could see how that drive was made and looked it all over — and boy, it just dawned on me right away, the way they were assembling this drive, it wasn't going to work!

I looked around and there wasn't a soul that I knew, and I couldn't tell millwrights from job supers or anybody else. I didn't know what to do. So I finally went back down to the office and found Oley. I told him, "You know, they're up there putting a drive on the drier section that isn't going to work the way they're doing it." I can remember seeing him, working on a bunch of papers at his desk and kind of shuffling them. He looked up at me out of the corner of his eye and he said, "Oh sure." Finally he said, "Well, let me get these papers straightened out and put away and we'll go up and have a look."

So we did go back up, and I said, "Now you step right up there and look at that machine and down into the basement where it's going to be hooked up, and you'll see what I'm talking about." And he did, and he said, "Oh my God!"

So my mechanical knowledge was really paying off: I had picked up something on a huge big machine, one that I didn't know anything about and had never seen before. In a few minutes, Oley had gotten on the telephone and called engineering, and there was a whole bunch of what I later would be calling white shirts on the job. These were engineers and supervisors who had to make a big decision on how this was all going to be handled, how it was going to be done over. But the thing that I came away with was that I had earned my pay the first day on the job, and that felt pretty good.

I soon discovered, however, that I had taken all of my reading and writing problems with me to this job. No matter how exciting it was and how I loved the job, I was in trouble. Engineers have to write — letters, memos, progress reports, requisitions — and I couldn't tell anybody that I couldn't write them. So I had to find a system that would work so that nobody would know that I couldn't write, and my secret wouldn't get out, that I had all kinds of literacy problems, because I was very ashamed of this, and I couldn't even talk about it with anybody. I was up to my old tricks, finding ways to accommodate or to get around my difficulties with language.

What happened in the mill was that another engineer in that office, in the construction department, happened to be a farm boy from Mississippi, and the two of us hit it off real well. He was an older engineer than I was; I was in my late 20s at the time. So Eddie and I became partners.

Because there were two of us working together, we could have our choice of the jobs that we wanted. We could pick off the best and the most interesting jobs, and we ran for several years very successfully. I worked out with the crews and loved it; I was on a transit or whatever had to be done in the field. When it came time to do reports and writing, Eddie didn't mind one bit being in a nice warm dry office doing that part, and I was out in the field doing the part that I loved. Our jobs were all coming in on time and under budget, and people around the mill were beginning to notice that. We made a very good team. But nobody ever knew that it had gotten set up because I couldn't write.

I am so spatial and so mechanical that I could anticipate problems with our machinery and figure out why things were going bad, and I really became a trouble-shooter. It got to the point where, when other jobs and other groups were having troubles with something, they would call down to the office to see if Harry could come up and give them a hand, and oftentimes I could find solutions. After a while, though, I came to the fact that Eddie was getting promoted all over the place and I wasn't. What was happening was, I wasn't leaving any paper trail. If I had understood about it and known how important that was, I'm sure that we could have changed the job reports and other papers so that my name would have been on them, too; but it was just an oversight and I didn't even think about it. I came to the conclusion that if I was going to have a real career, I'd have to do something else besides being in the paper mill.

There is no place that the Peter Principle kicks in faster than when a person in the workplace has a learning disability. For example, a man may be an excellent maintenance man, because he can fix anything, come up with solutions to problems, be very innovative and successful in his work. Because of that success, he gets promoted into a management slot — foreman, supervisor, crew chief. In his new job, he is responsible for lots of paperwork — filling out requisitions, doing time sheets, writing personnel reports. He cannot handle the paperwork. And he cannot share with anyone the fact that he cannot read and write to the necessary degree.

After a few such experiences, he learns to do something to avoid getting promoted. Perhaps he will just quit a job when a promotion is offered, or he'll do something to get fired. He'll do anything necessary to keep his disability a secret, to keep from being embarrassed. In my case, having Eddie to do all our paperwork let me keep my secret – but it also kept me from even being offered a promotion, and from having a chance to grow in my job.

I was so ashamed of my literacy problem that I did everything I needed to do to keep it a secret. I didn't want people to know how "dumb" I was. I covered up the fact that I couldn't read well and couldn't spell and write. I did everything I needed to do so that nobody would find out these horrible truths. As I look back at all of this, I can see that keeping that secret was more disabling than the disability.

Before I resigned from the mill, I got a job in a small metal finishing plant in Massachusetts. So Janet and I moved the whole family to Massachusetts and started on a new career. After two or three years, my uncle and I bought the plant out, and I acted as plant manager and plant engineer. I didn't have any particular written language demands, so that I could do things just about the way I wanted. What I did was, I ran the plant not from a desk, but from the floor. I worked right with the crews, and I could do the jobs in the plant. If I had to train somebody new, I didn't have to tell him how to do the job, I could show him. No lengthy instructions – I'd say, "This is the way we polish a plate," and demonstrate, or "This is the way we do electroplating" and do that. We also did cold rolling of steel, and I became very good at being able to change rolls and polish rolls and even do things faster, cheaper and better than they had been done previously.

We lived in Massachusetts from 1960 until 1973. During that time, our three children were educated in the Westborough schools. We considered it a very good educational system. However, two of our children should have had some services for their language difficulties, and it never happened. I don't know whether the school at that time didn't have any knowledge about learning disabilities or just kept very quiet about it,

27

because we never had the opportunity or the knowledge to get involved and do something about their language problems. I have always felt bad that I wasn't able to help my children, but I didn't know anything about it. By the time our grandchildren went to school (our grandchildren had some difficulties, too) we were ready.

After our children were in school full time, Janet went back to school to complete her education. She went to Worcester State College and ended up a teacher. She got a job in the Westborough school system; she taught the first grade for six years before we moved back to Maine.

It happened that the year that she started to teach, the school that she was in went to a new reading system called Keys to Reading. It was a very phonetic program with some multi-sensory portions to it, and Janet became very interested in reading and in teaching reading and the kids who had troubles learning to read, so this was the beginning of her understanding and interest in alternative reading programs. That program in that school was so successful in teaching reading that the state officials from Massachusetts came out to look at the school to see why their reading scores were so high. But for some reason, over the years the program got dropped. We've never understood why. Janet's early experience and interest were a tremendous help when we started looking at language and teaching in the LD field many years later.

After thirteen years, everything had worked well, but we still wanted to come back to Maine (and that seems to be a normal route for people that grow up in Maine – they may work out of state for a while, but they do tend to drift back). For us, thirteen years and we decided that we were ready to come back. So we sold out in Massachusetts and bought an old farm in Maine.

Being a farm boy, I thought that I would like to do some farming, and because I had been building boats in Massachusetts as a hobby, I wanted a nice shop so that I could build a few boats in the winter time to keep myself busy. We jacked up a barn and put a foundation under it and concrete floors in it;

we designed and built our own home; built the shop; and started out farming. We were raising cattle for beef and selling beef by the side to people with home freezers and had a good market established. The thing that really messed things up was that I did start building a few boats in the winter time, to keep busy, and that business took right off on us. I had to decide what I was going to do, whether I was going to farm or build boats; there was so much work that I couldn't do both.

We decided that the best way for us to earn a living on a farm was to build boats. So we leased out our fields and I began to build the boats full-time. This is where I really found a place for me to operate successfully and use my spatial-mechanical skills. I didn't understand about all of this at the time, but now, looking back at it, I can see how that all worked. I like to share that story of building the boats, because it demonstrates how a person with good spatial abilities can operate.

While I was still in Massachusetts, my friend Bob Brown got me interested in sailing. I bought a sailboat and taught myself to sail, and was really enjoying it. Bob was telling me about a boat in their family boathouse up here in Maine that was a real antique boat and had real nice lines. He asked if we could take a mold off from that boat and build ourselves each a boat just like it with a fiberglass hull. He bugged me about it for a long time, and finally I told him, "Why don't you bring the boat down and I'll have a look at it, and we'll see what we can do."

When the boat showed up, it was a very delightful old-style boat that had nice lines, and I could see why he was so excited about it. It was a 12-foot rowboat, still with most of its original trim. Bob knew that it was almost a hundred years old, so it was a boat reminiscent of the late 1800s or early 1900s. We didn't know anything about what kind of boat it was. It had been stored for years on its side and was all out of shape, so I took it over to my plant and straightened it out and put it all back into what its original shape was, or what I thought it was.

When you build a boat with a fiberglass hull, there are two ways to do it. You can build a plug (a full-size model, of wood and other materials) and apply the fiberglass coating to that, or you can use an existing hull, as we did with these boats. When you have a hull, you get it perfectly smooth, wax it (so the fiberglass won't stick to it), then build up layers of fiberglass saturated with resin to make the mold. After the fiberglass hardens, it will separate from the waxed hull. With this project, it was the third try when we finally made it, but we did get a mold and were able to make ourselves each a boat as he had suggested. The boats were white; we trimmed them out with varnished mahogany and made them look so fancy that commercial fishermen on the coast told us they looked pretty yachty.

The Maine coast was where we started rowing our new boats, because they were salt-water boats, high-sided and stable enough to handle ocean waves. We enjoyed trying them out in the open ocean. One day, after we brought them back into the launch area and pulled them up on the grass, an old-timer came along and looked them all over, and finally he said, "You know, those are a couple of pretty good-looking Whitehalls."

That was the first time I knew what these old boats were. From that lead, we learned their history and how far back they went and the different sizes that were made and what they were used for, and became quite interested in the whole project. I built several more 12-foot Whitehalls while I was in Massachusetts. When I turned my hobby into a business in Maine, I soon wanted other sizes, and I not only wanted rowboats but I wanted sailboats like they were originally. I knew the types of sails that they used and how they were made and what the spars looked like and how the rigging should be designed.

So this is where I started using my spatial ability. Because I was working with fiberglass and not wood, there are many things that I could do with shapes in glass that I couldn't possibly do with wood (because I couldn't make wood bend into the compound curves that I needed). So with the fiberglass, I wanted to take full advantage of the freedom of shape. I could make the bow of the boat much sharper, so that it would go through the water more easily. I could taper the stern below the water line, so that the water flow would be smoother and the boat would move with less effort. I could make the bottom of the boat flatter, and I could turn up the sides more abruptly, to make the boat more stable and provide more capacity. I kept the same overall dimensions as the original Whitehalls, and the same distinctive shape of the transom. I ended up with a low-maintenance boat that was lighter and cheaper than the originals.

I found that I could do all of this design work in my head. I could think about the boats the way I wanted to do them and I could actually see them in my mind. I could also put seats in and change them and move them around; I could put different kinds of sail rigs on and see what they looked like and get the proportions right and even tell how big the sails should be. And I could do this over long periods of time, and it was exciting to see these boats come into view for me. I could see the boats so plainly that every detail could be worked out. And with this huge amount of complicated data, I had no memory or recall problems — I could keep it, store it over a long period of time, bring it down and it would be correct and the latest version. Somebody asked me one day why I didn't use a CAD (computer-aided design) program to design the boats, and my answer to him was, "Why bother?" since I enjoyed doing it in my head.

Things like the sail can be shown on a flat piece of paper — I could draw out the sails and the sail rigs on paper — but the hull itself is a whole series of compound curves, and it's difficult to show that on a flat piece of paper. But I could see the boat in my head so plainly that I could carve a model of it to scale. Because a boat is symmetric, I had to carve only one side, and I came up with what is called a *half-hull*. If you go to a marine museum, you'll see many, many half-hulls displayed, and I know exactly how the minds of those people who did that worked, and I was able to do the same thing.

After the hull was carved, all I had to do was take the dimensions off it with a caliper and I had the information I needed to build the full-sized boat. There are lots of steps and they take months and months of work, but the thing of it was, I really enjoyed doing this work, and I didn't even think about it as work. For me, it was fun, and I could hardly wait some mornings to get down in the shop and to be working on the tooling and eventually to build the first boats. It was pretty exciting when I pulled the first boat up out of a new mold, to get to see just exactly what it looked like. Of course it would look exactly like the boat that I had envisioned in my mind, months before. I have now learned that there are lots of people that wouldn't be able to do this, and it has come as a shock to me, because I figured that anything I could do, anybody could do.

I had decided early that in building the boats I didn't want to hire a crew to do the work. I wanted to do it myself. I had been in charge of a crew once and didn't want to do it again. As my business grew, I developed a system of subcontractors to do parts of the work. This was what we would now call outsourcing. Two of those people were operating with small shops, doing most of the work themselves, or maybe a son would be helping them part-time. The man that ended up doing my fiberglass work was wonderful for me to work with. He understood how I wanted to do things, and he and I conversed so easily that we were able to solve problems and work up techniques and find ways that the boats could be molded the quickest and the easiest and the best. When I had suggestions or things that I wanted to tell him, in just a few words he would understand exactly what I was thinking, and he could even help develop the best systems for doing things. I was completely amazed at how easily he and I could talk to each other and how we both understood how the molding worked and the boats could be made. Working with him was extraordinarily productive, and I enjoyed it.

Another interesting part of that relationship was, he was so disorganized and had so much trouble keeping his work going that he hardly could manage his business. If he hadn't been scared to death of his bookkeeper, I don't think he could have managed it at all. His troubles were a lack of what we call *executive function* abilities — managing money, managing time, keeping schedules, and making your life mesh with other people's lives. I had a good understanding of these difficulties, and we worked up a system. I gave him just enough money to buy materials, and he knew that I was going to show up on Friday afternoon, with a check, to pick up hulls. So he would manage to get those boats out, because he would want some money for the weekend. With this system, we did business for a lot of years.

I eventually talked with him about learning disabilities, and he did say that he had had all kinds of troubles in school and that it sounded like the kinds of troubles that I'd had. He was very gifted in his spatial abilities, and that fit right along with my abilities, and that is why we were able to work together and enjoy doing it. In addition to his spatial abilities, he had very strong musical abilities and played professionally. He played the guitar and he could read music. He tried to explain it to me, but it didn't work for me at all. One of the interesting things was that he said he couldn't teach his brother, who was also a good musician, how to read music, but the brother could play and remember the music and reproduce it with no trouble at all. In fact, he said his brother sounded better than he did, even though he couldn't read music. These are examples of other very strong abilities, and of the kinds of talent that formal education over-looks.

The other man I worked with told me that he had gone to vocational school and had liked it and had done well. But when he got through school, he was very disappointed that he couldn't pass his certification test, and wasn't able to get the kinds of jobs that he should have been able to with vocational training. He was a machinist and did automotive work. He did work part of his life as a millwright, but ended up with his own shop, doing boat repair work. He repaired hulls and did inboard and outboard motor work. He and I worked very well together; he did assembly work for me, putting the boats together. It seems that those of us with learning disabilities are able to understand each other and function well together.

The boat business has now been sold to a young man who enjoys doing the same kind of work that I did. It made a very good living for me for 25 years, and I did lots of exciting things. It was a very special little niche in the boating business. I advertised nationally and sold boats all over the country, once hauling one as far as Alaska. Janet and I did a lot of traveling and did boat shows and met many, many wonderful people. The new boat owner, being a young man and thinking a little differently than I did, has put up a web page (www.bns-whitehall.com), and he told me recently that he has sold so many boats that he's had to return some deposits.

Understanding My Own
Learning Disabilities

Back when I was in my early 50s, my wife read a story in the *Reader's Digest* about dyslexia. She said that it sounded to her like the kinds of troubles I had, and it explained a lot of my difficulties. We went over the story together, and boy, it rang a lot of bells for me. It sounded exactly like the kinds of things that had been hampering me. I wanted to learn more about these difficulties in language, and we discovered that there were a couple of organizations working in Maine that dealt with what we wanted to find out about. One of them was Adults and Children with Learning Disabilities, which is now LDA, the Learning Disabilities Association of America; the other was the Orton Dyslexia Society, now called the International Dyslexia Association (IDA). We found that the two groups were running a joint state conference at the University of Southern Maine, and we went to that. We got lots of new information, and for the first time in my life I met other people that understood the issues I was trying to deal with. It was a life-changing event for me.

I was very surprised about all this, because I thought that I was the only one in the world that had these difficulties, and didn't know that as much as 10% of our population was involved. I had never met a single person that said, "I am learning-disabled or dyslexic," so that I didn't know that it was such a widespread condition. The more I learned, the more I wanted to learn about these language issues, so one day my wife and I went up to the University of Maine at Orono, to the bookstore, and found a couple of books on learning disabilities. One of them had come from Great Britain; it was sort of a textbook that talked about learning disabilities and dyslexia and the kinds of things that you could do about it. We went through that book and found it very interesting.

The second book was by Helene Simpson. She has learning disabilities, and she was telling her own story about going to school and the difficulties she had with teachers. It couldn't help but come across with all of the feelings involved in school failure and how we got treated. All of a sudden, it brought up all kinds of bad feelings in me that I didn't even know were there, and my whole world came tumbling down on top of me. I had always thought that I was a tough guy who didn't have feelings. Now I was in an emotional crisis; I was crying, and I was hurting, and I was scared, and I didn't know what was happening. It was a very, very traumatic experience.

I instinctively knew that I needed to have some help with all this, and that help needed to be in the form of counseling. This was an area that I hadn't really thought was particularly valuable in this world, but now I knew that I needed it. I made an appointment with the minister at church, and went in and sat there in his office and told him the story about what I had learned about learning disabilities and what had happened to me. I was telling him a story that I hardly believed myself, but he did believe me, and we talked about it for a long time. He finally said that he wasn't able to take on any more counseling work, but that he would be able to find somebody for me. He said he would do that as quickly as he could. I was pretty anxious to get some help, because I was still hurting badly and needed to get started. I've always been very grateful that he had taken the time and interest and believed me, so that I was able to get started.

In a few days, I was set up with a counselor. My counselor turned out to be an Episcopal priest that was doing counseling part time. His name is Geoff Robbins. It didn't take long for him to help me divide up the issues that I had to deal with so that they became manageable. I didn't know an awful lot about feelings and how you handle them and what they are and what can be done about it, and he was very good in that area. I don't think that he knew an awful lot about learning disabilities, but I did know something about that area. Between the two of us, we figured the whole thing out. We clicked very well together. It wasn't long before I felt much better and was learning again, and the more I learned, again, the more I wanted to know.

After a while, I was talking with Geoff about not knowing who these other people with learning disabilities are or anything about them, and I felt that I needed to do that. His first suggestion was, "Why don't you join a support group and get to meet other people who have these kinds of things and know what they're like and associate with them?" That sounded pretty good to me. I had a newsletter from the Learning Disabilities Association with some names of people that were working with adults, and one night I started calling them.

The first one I talked to was a woman on Long Island that understood me and understood all of my problems and understood exactly where I was coming from and what I needed. She had serious learning disabilities and hadn't been able to learn to read. One of her big problems was that she didn't know what to do with her mail when she got it – she couldn't even sort out the junk mail from the good mail and didn't know what to throw away. She had been remediated and was now reading; in fact, her remediation had been so successful that she was teaching other people to read. One thing that she was doing was running a support group for adults, and that was exactly what I needed, but I couldn't see any logistical way that, living in Maine, I could go to a support group meeting on Long Island. It was a very nice conversation, talking with somebody who had the same troubles that I did. It would have been nice to have gone to that support group, but not possible.

The second person I talked to was a woman by the name of Dale Brown in the Washington, D. C., area. In spite of her learning disabilities, she was a government employee, and was also working as a volunteer with other people that had learning disabilities. Later I was to serve on the Board of Directors of the Learning Disabilities Association of America with this woman. She also understood my needs and what I should do or how I should proceed, but it wasn't going to be possible for me to go to Washington to go to support group meetings. And I remember that she wished me well that night and hoped I would find something.

When I reported back to Geoff the troubles I was having finding a support group meeting, he didn't bat an eye. He said, "Well, what you need to do is start one, then." And he said, "I'll help you do it."

The two learning disabilities groups in Maine were able to help me round up half a dozen other people who had learning disabilities. We started to meet at my house, once a month, and Geoff became the facilitator for the group. For the first time, it really sank in that I was not alone. These folks all had the same kind of troubles I had. They'd had the same difficulties with their education and with relationships, and I was really learning from other people that had had the same kinds of experiences as I had.

The group went along well for a few months. Then, one night just before the meeting was to start, Geoff called and said he had an emergency and couldn't come. I had to pinch-hit as the facilitator that night, and I was off and running with a support group that I was facilitating. We all learned from each other, not only about learning disabilities but about compensatory kinds of things that we could do to help ourselves.

After a few months, we were able to reserve a conference room at the local hospital in Waterville to hold our meetings. This location gave us more space and made us feel more professional, and it was also easier to find. We started picking up new members. After about a year, somebody in the group said they thought this was all very valuable, the things that we were learning and talking about, and that the public should know more about it. So they suggested that we have a public meeting on learning disabilities. We all agreed that was a good idea, and because I was the facilitator for the group, I said I would find a place to hold this meeting. We set up with the school in Winslow for a meeting space, and we put a little notice in the paper that we were holding this meeting on learning disabilities. Janet and I arranged to have Rob and Linda, two officers from Maine LDA, come in as guest speakers.

Much to our surprise, that night about 60 people showed up. Some of them were adults with learning disabilities, who later became part of our support group. Several parents who were having trouble with their children in school also showed up. They didn't understand what the difficulties were, and the schools didn't seem to either. In addition to Rob's and Linda's presentations, I spoke on my learning disabilities. This was the first time in public for me, and I was only going to speak for about 10 minutes. It was a most difficult thing for me to do, but I did manage, and got through the evening, scared half to death.

This experience was another step on my unintended trip into the learning disabilities field. For the previous year, I had been talking easily about my learning disabilities with Geoff and the other people in the support group. But for this project, my name was in the paper with the fact that I had learning disabilities. Being so much more public than I had ever been before gave me lots of uncertain feelings. No one commented to me about seeing my name in the paper, and the people who came to the Winslow meeting were sympathetic and supportive, so the whole thing ended up being a positive experience for me.

After the meeting in Winslow, talking with Linda and Rob, I was telling them that I would like to get evaluated, and asking how could I do that and who would do it. They were working with me in the learning disabilities area at the time and didn't think it would be appropriate for them to do the evaluations, so they recommended Tri-Services in Maryland.

The other thing that they pointed out was that we had a lot of parents there that night who were in need of services, and they asked me if I would start a local chapter for parents, which I said I would do. Janet and I did that together, and we had a real active chapter going very quickly.

From all of the studying I had done, I understood that I had learning disabilities, but I didn't know exactly how disabled I was, and I didn't know exactly what areas the disabilities came in. Perhaps, still, I even needed to have absolute, official proof that I was learning-disabled. I was at the point where I really wanted to be evaluated, and the referral to Tri-Services was just what I needed. In the fall of 1987, I made an appointment for a full-scale, comprehensive evaluation. Tri-Services was in Chevy Chase, Maryland, just outside of Washington, and we had friends in Springfield, Virginia, about 45 minutes away, with whom we could stay. The plan was that we would stay two or three days in Springfield, and I would have the evaluation. It was going to take Tri-Services several days to write up the evaluation and report on it, so Janet and I would go down to Williamsburg, Virginia, for a few days for a vacation and a chance to do some exploring. Then we would come back and review the evaluation at Tri-Services.

I thought this would all be quite routine, but as the time neared, I found that I got very nervous about the whole thing. We were there early enough so that I could find the location a day ahead of time. The next morning I was off early to be evaluated. When I got there, in addition to doing evaluations at this location, they had a school for children that had learning disabilities, so there were a lot of children playing outdoors. I was finding it difficult to go in. I was finding all kinds of excuses and reasons why I didn't really need to. But I did go in, and I did really have to put one foot ahead of the other to get myself in there.

Once I was in there and started meeting and talking with people who understood my difficulties, I felt very comfortable. And some of the tests, like the ones testing spatial ability, were no problem at all. However, on the tests in the language areas, I knew that I was failing terribly, and I did find that very difficult.

Susan Jenkins, a Ph.D. psychologist, and Diane Campbell, an educational diagnostician, did my evaluation. It was a series of tests, one right after another, all day long. They started out being rather broad, and as Susan and Diane figured out the areas that I was having difficulty with, they gave me sub-tests to cover those particular areas. Even though I was an adult, I was being tested in a lot of the same areas children are.

The tests were things like reading a couple of paragraphs and having to explain what the material was in there, sometimes doing it orally and sometimes written. These are the kinds of things that I have terrible struggles with and hadn't done much of because I didn't want people to know how much I struggled and how poor my abilities were in these areas. I was having to share with Susan and Diane all of the kinds of things that had bothered me so much for so many years. I discovered right away that these folks were really interested in understanding about me and were there to help me understand about my difficulties. They were supportive and even understood my difficulties way beyond what I did. This all made the whole process doable.

People like me have all kinds of problems with staying focused and have all kinds of distraction problems. One of the things that happened was that many of the tests were done in a soundproof room with double doors, so that there wasn't any kind of distraction from the outside world at all, which also helped. Another time, I was in an office where I was being tested, and the tester could hear a whole bunch of people talking in the hallway outside. She flew out of there to quiet them down so I wouldn't have to contend with that distraction.

In one of the tests, I was given information orally — mathematical problems with all kinds of numbers that I had to remember to solve the problem in my head and then give an oral answer. I was having a terrible time with it; I just couldn't seem to hold all those numbers and figure that all out in my head and then give an oral answer. I was telling them that I thought that I was pretty good in math and I was kind of discouraged taking this test, and they began to laugh and say that they weren't testing my math ability, they were testing my short-term memory ability.

The day was very hard, because many things that I was being asked to do were the exact things that I have so much trouble and struggle with. It was very tiring, and I was glad when the day was over. Even though this evaluation was difficult, and it cost me $1,000, I have always been very grateful for it. I think it is one of the best things that I have ever been able to do for myself.

After we did our sightseeing trip, we came back to go over the evaluation. Janet went with me for that part. The evaluation wasn't completely written up, but all of the test scores were completed, and they had a complete picture of where I stood in the learning disabilities or dyslexic area. One of the first things that Susan had to tell me was that my reading was at the 30th percentile rank. I can remember that hurt, because even though I have trouble with language, I understand numbers very well, and I knew exactly what that meant. And it does mean that I am reading way, way below what would be expected compared to my intelligence; 70 percent of the people in the United States can read better than I can. She spent some time with me, because she wanted me to really understand that I'm reading at the 30th percentile and what it means, and not to deny it or discount it.

The next thing that she had to tell me was that I'm spelling at the seventh percentile; that is, 93 percent of the population spells better than I do, and only six people out of 100 are worse spellers than I am. And this hurt even worse. It was hard for me to imagine that that was all I was doing. Susan was very determined that I would hear this, and not deny it. So she spent quite a lot of time talking about that and what it meant and how it had blocked me in doing so many things that I wanted to do.

An evaluation doesn't just check to see what the areas are that you're having difficulties with, it also checks your intelligence or general IQ. For that part, I discovered that my general intelligence is in the top 10 percent of the population. I think that it has been harder for me to understand that part than it was with the parts about where I was so low, because within all the language areas I had had all kinds of trouble and people explained to me very explicitly exactly how bad it was, and I had been criticized for my spelling and people had been impatient, so it wasn't difficult for me to understand that I did have troubles in those areas. But I didn't know where my special strengths were, and it has taken me a long time to find out about them.

Tri-Services determined how learning-disabled I was by various methods, including using the discrepancy formula. This method compares how well you do in areas of disability, like reading and spelling for me, against your general intelligence. It turned out that my general intelligence is in the top 10 percent of the population and some of my language difficulties are in the bottom 10 percent of the population. So you can't get much more discrepant than that. (Current research suggests that the discrepancy method is not the best way to decide if a person has learning disabilities. But it's a method that was used when I was evaluated and is still being widely used today.)

When we talk about learning disabilities, we're using it as a very broad term. It doesn't say what the disability is; it doesn't say whether it's in language or in math or in both. To actually understand where our disability is, we have to know what our specific learning disabilities are. I learned from my Tri-Services evaluation that I have five specific learning disabilities. I have problems with audio perception and visual perception (now called *auditory and visual processing*), short-term memory, word retrieval, and small motor activities.

Audio and visual perception

For me, audio perception means that I have real difficulty hearing language and understanding it in my brain. There is nothing wrong with my hearing, but to get the language from my ears into my mind I have to process that part. It takes time, and a lot of thought, to get a message. Sometimes people speak to

43

me and I won't be prepared and the message gets completely lost, so I have to ask for them to repeat. By being prepared, the next time around I can get the information.

Another part of this is what we now call *phonemic awareness*. This means that I don't get part of the bits and pieces of sounds that make up words. Lack of phonemic awareness causes us to have difficulties in reading and spelling. Because we can't hear all the sounds in words, we cannot easily see how the spelling and sounds match up. Once again, processing comes into play. Language does not automatically end up in my mind. To get it there takes time and work.

All this processing is a cognitive process, and it ties up my mind so that I can't be doing other tasks at the same time. Processing is often hindered by background noise — for example, people talking in a crowded room, traffic, and other outside noises. These sounds are all distracting, and I can't automatically shut them out. Any stress that I might be feeling — if I'm tired, nervous, or worried, for example — also compounds the problem.

For reading, visual perception is similar to audio perception, except that it is the process of seeing printed language and matching it up with sounds to make words. I had real trouble learning all those letters and letter combinations, and I still can't process them fast. It's not clear now whether my visual perception problems had a real impact on my learning to read or if it was mostly my language problems that made reading so hard. The processing involved in reading was just something that was always very difficult for me.

When I was in high school, I had to read a book and do a book report, like everybody does. I was very determined to read that book and do a book report like everyone else. I started reading the book after school every day until dinnertime, and then would read again in the evening. This went on I don't know how long, but for a long time, and I just couldn't seem to understand the book. I couldn't keep track of the story, and I couldn't even remember who all of the characters were and what the book was about. I ended up doing a book report on a little section of that book, and nobody caught on to what I did. I had the desire to read the book, put in the time and effort, and it just didn't work. The truth of the matter was that I didn't have any idea what that book was about, and I never did finish it.

After all these years and all of this experience, sometimes when I'm reading, I will still discover that whatever I'm reading doesn't make any sense to me. When I go back and check, I discover that there is a word that I have misread, and it has changed the meaning of the whole paragraph.

I have discovered that my visual processing requires more cognitive power than audio processing does. For me, I have discovered that subvocalizing (that is, while I am trying to read, quietly saying the language) makes it easier to understand what I am reading, because I am receiving language through my ears at the same time that I am receiving it through my eyes. This technique completely contradicts teachers' advice to young children not to move their lips as they learn to read.

One of the Tri-Services recommendations was that I use talking books. This was wonderful for me. For the first time, I could read a novel with my ears and understand the story (because I had enough cognitive power left over to follow the story). Some of the first books that I listened to were by Ernest Hemingway. After I had been listening to a book for some time, it dawned on me that the story was really Hemingway's personal story. I could see how he loved the café life and visiting and talking with friends, how he was kind of a rascal. This was a completely new experience for me, and I realized that this was the kind of thing that English teachers had talked about for many years, and I hadn't had a clue as to what they meant. A whole world of literature opened up for me.

I listened to all kinds of different novels, did several biographies, and I even listened to Dr. Ruth. I discovered from that book that there wasn't anything that you couldn't talk about, even learning disabilities. But I didn't know if what I was reading and seeing in books now was the same as what other people got out of books, and I all of a sudden wanted to take a literature course and talk with other people about what I was reading. So as I was lecturing around on learning disabilities, I was saying that I would like to take a literature course, and have the books all on tape and do it with other people that were doing the same thing, and if anybody was interested in teaching that kind of literature course, I would be their first student. Eventually, a woman said she'd like to teach that course, and I did go as the first student. We started out with two or three other students, but they didn't last too long. I did spend that winter going every week in the evening and doing books and listening to them on tape and having a discussion about them. It was just a further step for me in literature.

Short-term memory

My short-term memory problem means that I can't remember things like words, random numbers, people's names, grocery lists. I forget about chores that I'm supposed to do, and have trouble keeping track of time. One of the many things I couldn't do in school was copy material accurately — for example, an assignment written on the board. Since I've been working on learning disabilities, I've asked adults who don't have a learning disability what that process was like for them, to copy from the board onto a paper. Some tell me that they could take down three or four sentences into memory and reproduce them on paper without having to look back. I had another adult tell me that he could hold at least a paragraph from one reading and be able to put that down on paper. That process is something those of us who have a short-term memory disability could never experience.

I have watched people look up a telephone number in the book, close the book and put it away and then accurately dial the number. For me, I have to have the number right up beside the telephone, and the best I can do is retain three digits, and I have to subvocalize.

Lack of short-term memory is a nuisance in many ways in our

daily lives. I have trouble remembering appointments, remembering to do certain tasks, going to the store and bringing home three items or more. Janet would sometimes think I was pretty irresponsible for messing up buying a few groceries, and when I made the mistakes, I felt pretty irresponsible. Now that we both understand about short-term memory problems, I go to the store with a list and come home successful every time. Short-term memory plays an important part in what we call *executive function* abilities — the ability to be organized, keep your life on track, and get done the work that you intend to do.

Word retrieval

Word retrieval trips me up sometimes. This means that I can be talking on a subject and moving right along and get to a word that I want to use and it won't be there. Sometimes I can get around it by finding a substitute word that I can bring up, or if I work on it, I can sometimes get the missing word to come up. However, this can be a very annoying problem.

Names seem to be a bigger problem than random words. This is true of most people, I think, but my problem is worse than average. To help me remember names, I have learned to use associations, and sometimes I'm quite proud of myself. I remember meeting a man one day whose name was Carstetter. There was no way in the world that I could possibly remember this name, so my choice was "car starter." This wasn't the same name, but close. To me, a car starter was an old-fashioned crank that you stuck through the grille of an automobile just below the radiator, and you turned the engine over by hand until it started. This man wasn't an old crank, but close, and I still remember his name years later.

Another problem, one that I think is more directly related to learning disabilities, is that I tend to forget words that I haven't used on a regular basis. While I was a sailboat designer and builder, I learned the language involved specifically for sailboats. I spent a lot of time learning all of that language and all about sailboats, so that, when I talked, the language would come easily. For many years I did boat shows and spent my days talking with customers about sailboats, and I wouldn't have any trouble; I stayed quite fluent. But certain times of the year, I spent more time building boats and didn't talk with people about them; and if somebody wanted to talk in specific boating terminology, I wouldn't have that language up and I couldn't use it. So I would get the person to talk more about the boat, and they would use the specific terms and names, and all of a sudden that language would flow back for me and I would be off and working okay.

Small motor

Small motor problems (and large motor problems) often accompany learning disabilities. Large motor problems affect your ability to walk, run and jump; small motor problems affect your ability to make fine movements and do small, intricate tasks. My evaluation didn't include any tests for large motor problems, but I know I have them. I'm not good at sports, and I often feel like a klutz when I move.

Small motor problems supposedly make it hard to do any kind of fine work, but I have found that I can use my hands for many tasks. As a child, I was building balsa-wood model airplanes, and spending hours and hours building objects with an erector set very successfully, and loving it. My boat-building required both small-motor and large-motor skills, and I had no problems with that. My small-motor problem seems to be limited to what is called *dysgraphia*, and is probably related to my trouble with reading and spelling. What it means is that I am one of the world's messiest writers. As a child in school, I could never satisfy a teacher with my handwriting. My hand simply would not make the letters the way I wanted it to. Even today, I can't write myself a note that I can read tomorrow. Dysgraphia can become a serious block for writing. For those of us with dysgraphia, we never have developed automaticity in writing. We continue to process how the letters are shaped. For me, I continually have to tell my fingers how to write. It still is a processing procedure or a cognitive procedure (a thinking process).

We left Washington in the fall of 1987 with a lot more knowledge about my learning disabilities. The people at Tri-Services spent several hours with us, helping us to understand what the evaluation was saying and what it meant for me. It was important for me to understand these difficulties, but it was also very important for Janet to understand them, too. It helped us both. I see this evaluation as being a real turning point for me in understanding about learning disabilities and more specifically my own learning disabilities. It opened up another whole new project or process in understanding exactly where my disabilities are and how I can cope with them and use this information to make my life easier and better.

Putting My LD Experience
to Work for Others

In the fall of 1987, Janet and I started working to put together a local chapter for the the Maine branch of the Learning Disabilities Association, which was then called Adults and Children with Learning Disabilities. Janet had become interested in the learning disabilities field and was learning right along with me. It was natural for her to do this, because she was a teacher and had been taking special courses in reading and understood some of the needs of children that have language difficulties.

We started holding monthly meetings and advertising them in the local newspaper. It was surprising how many people started coming. At first most of them were parents whose children were having trouble in school, and who didn't know exactly what the problems were or what the solutions were, but thought maybe we could help. Then we started getting more and more service providers — teachers at first, and then administrators, counselors, all kinds of people who wanted to help children. A few adults would come to the local chapter, too, to learn about their own learning disabilities, and we would steer them to the adult support group.

At most meetings we would have a speaker, and Janet had started gathering up materials on all aspects of learning disabilities, and we had lots of handouts. As people started coming, some of them were very interested and came on a regular basis. We started putting them to work, and after a few months we had a real working organization. There was a real need to assist parents. The more we worked, the more calls we started getting, and it started growing automatically. Janet and I both continued to learn about learning disabilities and the needs, and I started speaking publicly about learning disabilities, and the project kept growing.

After about a year and a half, the people that were at the state level decided that they just couldn't go on any longer, because they were so busy they couldn't keep up. They were going to resign their positions as board members and officers of the Learning Disabilities Association, and they asked me if I would become the state president. My first reaction was no, that I hadn't been a local chapter president long enough to get well established and that's what I was doing and what I should keep on doing. However, after some thought, I did decide that I was ready to move up. The last action of the state people was to appoint me the new state president. I ended up being president without a board, without any officers; I was a single person with no organization. Luckily, Janet agreed to help me. If we hadn't done this as a team, it would never have happened.

One of the first things that we did was go see Peter Stowell at the Maine Developmental Disabilities Council (DD Council). We told him our story about what we were doing and what we wanted to do and asked if there would be any help for us to do it. He gave us $600, and this was just enough for us to get started; it helped pay for materials and the telephone bill. Janet put together packets of materials, and every time anyone called looking for information she would send out all the information they wanted, and more. We started getting calls from all over the state, and at about that time we started traveling all over the state to do workshops on learning disabilities. We ended up doing speaking engagements two or three times a week.

There was a real need to expand our services, because parents were having so much difficulty. The Maine Parent Federation (a private nonprofit organization headquartered in Gardiner) offered us some office space and agreed to help us expand and get some funding. We brought together some of the people who were really working and were interested in learning disabilities to meet with David Stockford, the state Director of Special Education. He told us that night if we would put together a group that represented the whole State of Maine, he would be interested in funding the work that we were doing. We put together a board and officers, and the Maine Department of Education gave us a $20,000 grant to start. Janet became the executive director of the Learning Disabilities Association of Maine.

We discovered early on that the parents were having all kinds of troubles getting appropriate services for their children in school. People were coming to us with stories about their children not wanting to go to school, in tears over problems at school, failing courses and not getting specific help from the school on how to solve these problems. At that time, we had laws in place that set up special education, and the parents had definite rights and protections. But they wouldn't know anything about these issues. It seemed to be our job to teach about learning disabilities and the difficulties that learning disabilities present in school, to teach the parents to become advocates for their children and to understand what their needs were and how the process worked with the educational system to get appropriate services for their children.

It wasn't long before we discovered that the schools didn't really know how to provide the kinds of services these children needed. So we made a decision not to work just in advocacy, but to teach everyone involved about learning disabilities and how to deal with the issues successfully. By the time I became state president, we had been working with adults long enough to have a pretty good idea about how all this should be done. One of our methods was to use the educational consultants we had found to work with adults and bring them into Maine schools to teach teachers about reading programs and show them the techniques that will work for people who struggle in language. We first started training individual teachers, who found it difficult to go back to their school systems and introduce a new or different type of program. In the last few years, we have been working with groups of teachers and sometimes whole school systems, and this has been much more effective.

It wasn't difficult to do all this, because there were many teachers who were interested in our methods and wanted to become trained. They, just like the parents, were frustrated by some children's inability to learn the same way as other children learned. Since we have shown them some new approaches and techniques, we have sat in classrooms and watched teachers instruct students with learning disabilities to read, write, and spell, and it has been very effective.

I remember a reading class in a classroom that was all second-grade students with learning disabilities. The teacher used several different techniques; in one of them, she was using flash cards and the students, one at a time, were giving the sound for the group of letters on the cards. She held up a card for a little girl, and the little girl's answer wasn't right, so the teacher helped walk her through the sound that she was sup- posed to give for those letters. The teacher even told her how to hold her mouth and where her tongue should be, and after a few minutes, the little girl got it right. And the teacher said, "That's good, and I'm going to hold your card out, so that we'll try it again in a little while." The next time the teacher held the card up, the little girl got it much quicker, but did still struggle some. The third time the teacher held up the card, the answer was loud, clear and correct, and her classmates cheered. What a sight to see the class support for this student, as well as the support from the teacher! This was a very long way from anything that I had ever experienced in school, and also a long way from any student who was failing because of ineffective techniques.

To watch the success and the support of everybody involved was an extreme emotional experience for me. A few minutes later, Janet and I were in a conference room with the building principal, some special education teachers, a counselor and an educational consultant. The counselor asked me how I felt watching this program, and I uncontrollably burst into tears. Everybody was a little nervous and uneasy, but I soon got over it, and we had our discussion about the program and how effective it was and how it could be expanded.

I later asked the consultant if they understood why the tears. Her reply was that there wasn't anything that I could have said that would have been more effective for them. After that, she said, whenever they were discussing the program and trying to figure out the best things to do, somebody would ask, "Well, what would Harry say?"

We ended up with a whole group of consultants who brought in all kinds of effective reading programs that were appropriate. No one program would work for every child with learning disabilities, but with so many new choices, teachers could find something for almost every student. Eventually, we would bring in as many as a dozen consultants at our annual state conferences and run a full day of introductory trainings to all of these various programs. As many as 200 teachers would sign up and give us $100 apiece to take the day's training.

In Maine, as well as in other states across the country, these reading programs have advanced to the point where some schools are beginning to arrange for their own training and are making the necessary changes. We still have lots of schools to go, but we have started a process towards change.

In addition to this work, Janet and I started doing talks on learning disabilities for anybody that asked anywhere in the state. We ended up being out two or three nights a week. We did things like in-service trainings for vocational schools, Literacy Volunteers and foster-parents (a high percentage of youngsters in foster care have learning disabilities, we discovered) and the state vocational rehabilitation program. We put together a traveling mini-conference, using the same people each time. One was a legal advocate, one an educational consultant, one a parent; and I spoke on what it's like to live with learning disabilities. We also had a speaker from the local area. This was a fun project, and we moved it around the state to places that wouldn't normally have a conference; we went Down East and up in The County. (For non-Mainers, Down East is Washington County, Maine's easternmost county, and The County is Aroostook County, the state's northernmost and largest county, both very rural areas.)

While all this was happening, I was getting asked to present in schools, sometimes to do an in-service for teachers, but often to talk with the students about learning disabilities. I did many grade schools, high schools, vocational schools, and universities and colleges.

I was there for several reasons. One of them was to help with the friction between the students in special education and those in regular education. In many schools, there was harassment and teasing among students, and the plan was that if I would get up and say that I had learning disabilities, it would give the whole school population a lot better idea about the difficulties, and the solutions, for the special education students. Lots of times, the gymnasium would be set up with metal chairs, and a podium with a loudspeaker would be set up for me, and the whole school would file in. I did my regular talk about my disability and the difficulties that it had caused me and what I had learned about it. I told the students that we all have areas we have difficulties in. Mine happens to be language; for others, it might be mathematics, or sports, or music. But I promoted the general theme that we all have strengths and we all have weaknesses. The difference for those who are like me, who have trouble in language or math, is that we also have trouble in school, because so much school work requires language or math. Our differences become disabilities.

After I presented, I always would have a discussion period. Usually I could get a good discussion going, even with high-school kids. A lot of the questions would be real pertinent questions about education and how I had done specific things, but also some surprising things would happen. I frequently got asked how old I was, and did I color my hair.

One day, in front of several hundred high school kids, a

student asked me if I had ever considered suicide. With a question like this, you don't know exactly where it's coming from. My answer to him was that for me, it hadn't been a problem; however, it had been a problem for many of the people that I had worked with.

Another day, with a group of younger children, there were hands up all over the room during the discussion, and I started taking them one at a time. When I got to this particular student at the back of the room and asked him for his question, he couldn't remember it. I assured him it was all right and that I sometimes had those kinds of difficulties. I asked him to think about the question again, and when he remembered it to put his hand up and I'd call on him right away. In a few minutes his hand was back up, and I practically cut a kid off to get back to him. And his question was, did the other kids make fun of me in school? The room went to a dead silence, because everybody knew where that question was coming from. I told him yes, that other kids had made fun of me in school, and that it hurt and I didn't like it. One of the teachers told me afterwards that they were very surprised that he was able to ask that question.

A second major goal of my presentations was to get youngsters to open up and talk about their learning disabilities. Sometimes I would spend part or all of my time in a school talking just with students with learning disabilities; sometimes I would lead discussions with mixed groups, special and regular education students.

On a trip to The County, I ended up in Fort Kent at the high school. When I got there first thing in the morning, they were loading students on buses to go to the vocational school, and I was disappointed about that. But after they realized what I was going to say, they unloaded those students. So I had the whole high school for a general informational session on learning disabilities. It was a good session with lots of interaction.

After the high school session, busloads of kids started coming in from all over the district, and they were all identified as having learning disabilities. I spoke with them in groups of about 50. These kids were able to talk about learning disabilities and had good questions. But the thing that really stands out in my mind about those sessions is that the kids had never been together before as a group, and they were completely amazed at how many of them there were. They kept looking around and making comments about it. I think bringing these kids together as a group was one of the most productive things that happened that day. The last group I had, there was one kid who was very ADHD (hyperactive), and he kept asking me if the session was done. We were finishing up, and finally I said "Yes, we're all done." And he took right over and had those kids put the desks back in lines (we had arranged them in a big circle for our discussion) and got the room all squared away in nothing flat.

Another day, on one of the Maine islands, I had the whole high school. The school officials had decided that they wanted me to talk with the students about learning disabilities and to get them to open up and start discussing their learning disabilities or their experiences with other students with learning disabilities. The school felt the best way for that to happen would be for me to talk with the students without any other adults there. The only thing that they were going to do was to have their gym teacher there in case any discipline problems had to be dealt with. She was very young, and all of the students loved her, and the officials felt that her being there wouldn't interfere with their being able to open up. She stayed in the back so that she'd be somewhat out of sight. They put out the gym mats and we met on the gym floor, with the students lying any way they wanted on the mats. I sat on a mat in front of them all. We did get a very good discussion going, and there were a lot of students that said they were having difficulties. Some of them were receiving services and some weren't. It did open up a good dialogue with all of the students. And it happened that a lot of the students had learning disabilities.

(I have discovered that in very rural areas, such as a Maine island or up in The County, a lot more people seem to have learning disabilities. I wonder if what is happening is that, as families grow up in these areas, those who get successful educations tend to move away where they can get appropriate jobs, and those that have language troubles stay in their areas. I know that many people with learning disabilities can do a fantastic job in farming, commercial fishing, running machinery of all kinds, and generally being able to run small businesses.)

In that island school, we found a freshman who was having all kinds of trouble in school, and everybody was working with him and trying to help him. His mother was tutoring him from the time he got home from school until dinner, and then working with him again in the evening. He would have his lessons down perfect, and he was going off to school the next day to fail his exams. It was decided that Janet and I would meet with his parents that night, after I spoke. The parents were uncertain if their son should also attend. I said he certainly should, because he was old enough to know what his disabilities were and how to deal with them.

During our conversation that night, the parents explained how they had worked so hard with this young man, and he didn't seem to make any progress, and it was obvious that the whole family was very frustrated over this whole business. I asked the young man what he would like to have out of this meeting. His answer was, "I would like to have some time to ride my bicycle."

As we talked, we discovered that this young man was very musical. He was musical to the point that he could even compose. So that gave Janet and me a chance to start explaining to the parents and the student that he had an unusual talent, which no one was paying attention to or helping him develop. I think the parents began to see what was happening in a different light. We suggested that the school start testing him orally rather than in writing, and that's really all it took – he had been retaining his lessons, and all he needed was a different way to show what he had learned. He was able to put together a three-piece band at school and play at assembly some music that he had written. All this changed school tremendously for this young man. He also ended up with time to ride his bicycle.

Another day down on the Maine coast, I was going to talk at an elementary school. The school officials knew that I was a boat-builder and said that the children would be very interested in the boats and asked me to talk about that a little bit. So I showed up with some pictures and half-hulls. Once I started talking about the boats, I wasn't sure that we were ever going to be able to get to learning disabilities. When we finally did, because this was a younger group, they could talk more freely. There was a girl, probably only in the second or third grade, who talked about her disabilities. She had been taught enough so that she had a good understanding, and could give specific examples, and it was a real help — it set the tone for our discussion.

There also was a boy who was having difficulty because he wouldn't look at the teachers when they talked to him. We were able to talk about this in open discussion, and what was happening for him is what happens to a lot of us with learning disabilities. We have difficulty with verbal expression because we have to process the language so much to get it out of our mouths that any kind of a distraction blocks us from doing that. For many, to look at somebody is enough distraction to keep us from putting our language together. What we have to do is look somewhere else. It might be at the floor, or I have noticed that many need to look out a window; the blank light seems to help. I explained all of this to the group. I did acknowledge that it was difficult to talk with somebody that wouldn't look at you, but said that it was something that couldn't be helped and that they needed to understand. Also, the student needed to understand that it did bother other people. The way to start changing it all is to first find something that can be looked at which brings us around so that the other person can at least see our face. Eventually, a lot of us can look somebody in the face and keep a good conversation going. I talked with the teacher afterwards and explained all of this and suggested that she help by bringing the vision around more, so that she could first see the face, and eventually the boy might be able to look at her feet, and then at a button on her shirt.

During our discussion that day, the young man was always looking out the window, and it was distracting for me. So I set up a system with him that I would check with him from time to time to see if he was listening to me, and would he just wave. It worked; I felt more connected, and he was apparently following everything I had to say, because the minute I would say, "Wave," he would wave.

Janet and I spent about two years primarily focused on Maine, traveling around the state and meeting people that were interested in learning disabilities issues. It gave us an opportunity to learn about the needs of adults, children, parents and service providers such as teachers, counselors and administrators in the field. Because of our interest and need for information, we got in touch with other organizations that were participating in the learning disabilities field on the national level, to get pamphlets and good information for the people that we were dealing with. Our most important resource was the Learning Disabilities Association, because we had a definite tie to that group.

As the state president of LDA of Maine, I started going to national conferences. The first conference I went to was in Miami Beach, at a beautiful hotel right on the sand. Janet and I went together, and it was a wonderful opportunity to extend our knowledge about learning disabilities. We attended as many break-out sessions (simultaneous panels and workshops) as we could, listened to all of the keynote speakers, and were very fascinated by the whole experience. We not only got to learn a lot about learning disabilities, but we also got to meet and start to know some of the people at the national level. As a state president, I started getting acquainted with the presidents from the other states. It was all so very busy that we never did get out to the beach to go swimming. That's the way it seems to be with the folks at the Learning Disabilities Association; they are working so hard, and doing so many meetings and putting on so much program, that there is very little time for play.

After two or three years of going to the national conference, Dale Brown, who was on the board at the time and also on the nominating committee (and it is the same Dale Brown that I had talked with years before on how to get a support group going), asked if I would be interested in running for the board of the national organization. I had never imagined doing such a thing, but after giving it a little thought, I said yes.

I filled out all of the papers that are necessary to go to the nominating committee and was accepted as a candidate to be presented at the Assembly of Delegates at our next national conference. This is a pretty lengthy process. You have to have references, and you have to have recommendations, and you have to fill out a lot of papers to say what your views are, and give your ideas on lots of different hard questions. You also have to do a telephone conference interview with the nominating committee, who in turn keep asking you various questions to see what your views are. My name was submitted to the Assembly of Delegates along with the rest of the slate, and I was elected to a three-year term as a board member at our annual conference in February 1990.

Things started out in a hurry. Right away there were board meetings, and I was also going to be on a brand new committee called the Adult Issues Committee. This was set up to start dealing with the needs of adults and to serve that population more. This was a very natural place for me to be because, as an adult with learning disabilities, I know more about these problems than a lot of other people would. After a couple of years, I was made chairman of the Adult Issues Committee. I had the responsibility for making that committee work and getting its assigned goals done.

One of the big projects we did during that time was to conduct an adult survey. The committee put together an extensive survey that touched on adults' lives in many ways, asking about their academic experiences, work, mental and physical health, and social and emotional issues. The survey was published in our newsletter, *Newsbriefs*, as a pull-out section and went out to all of the membership. It was many pages and very complex, and over 600 responses came back. Even though so much reading and writing was a struggle for those with language disabilities, people were eager to share their experiences and wanted to be part of solutions for adults. Many people wrote their own stories and sent them in; we compiled many, many pages of these stories. They were all dealing with the problems of having learning disabilities, and the failures, and just how hard it is to live in this society with a learning disability. It took months and months to handle all of the data. The final report was called "They Speak for Themselves," and it pointed out the need for adults to know and understand about their learning disabilities in order to have a more successful life.

In some ways, the self-selected people who answered the survey were not typical of the whole group of people with learning disabilities. For example, only 9% identified themselves as school dropouts, and almost half either had a college degree or were in college at the time. Very few — less than 10% — of the respondents reported drug or alcohol abuse problems. Three quarters had been employed or were employed, at least part-time. We did have to keep in mind that the people that had filled out this survey were the ones who knew about learning disabilities, because they were all people that had been exposed to the Learning Disabilities Association one way or another. The survey did not cover people that had no support or information.

Even these comparatively well-informed people reported many problems that they felt were linked to their learning disabilities. They especially felt the need for more help in getting and keeping appropriate jobs and in being able to explain their disabilities and get the accommodations they needed to be successful. The survey respondents also talked about their need for more education and for better social skills.

One thing I found very interesting was how much these people's experiences were like mine. Like me, they had gone through a whole lot of school failures — being told they were lazy and didn't try, being held back a grade, being told they didn't belong in college. When they wrote about their frustrations and humiliations, I knew just what they meant.

Due to the work of the adult section, the board could see how important it was to serve adults and how adults were really involved in the whole process. A few years later, the board changed LDA's structure to emphasize learning disabilities as a life-time condition, which I think was very appropriate. Learning disabilities don't go away; you still have issues that need to be dealt with, and as they're dealt with, life becomes a lot easier and more productive and more fulfilling. We need to have an understanding about learning disabilities in every phase of our lives.

The Learning Disabilities Association already had a good sound structure for working with children in kindergarten through twelfth grade and with their parents. Now the Association set up three more areas — one for adults, one for post-secondary students, and one for preschool children — each modeled after the kindergarten through twelfth grade program. So we had the full life covered. We set up new committees in each area, with a chairperson responsible for each particular area. Each committee started out with two or three subcommittees; since the initial organization, some have been added and some eliminated. In this way, LDA officially recognized that a learning disability was a lifetime condition, and we were going to bring services to everybody involved.

We have made lots of progress in getting people to understand adults with learning disabilities, what their needs are, and some of the things that can be done to help. However, I have been disappointed in the fact that more people with learning disabilities haven't been able to assume leadership responsibilities. I know that this is a time when volunteerism is not as popular as it used to be, and it's difficult to man volunteer organizations with good leadership people. However, I do know that nobody understands an adult with learning disabilities any better than another adult with learning disabilities. I think this is one of the things that we really need in this field. We can use a lot of adults in areas like supporting substance abuse programs and literacy programs, disseminating information, and training or educating new recruits to become part of a nationwide network to bring more knowledge to the whole field.

I served three years on the LDA board and was reelected to a second three-year term. At the same time, I was elected by the board to be the board liaison to the executive committee. I did this for two years, and gradually became more involved with management of the organization and had to turn over some of my committee work to others. After two years on the executive committee, I was elected treasurer by the Assembly of Delegates and stayed on the executive committee. This was really a good spot for me to be, because I am a businessman and have had experience in running organizations from a financial point of view.

After two years as treasurer, several people were encouraging me to run for president. There was some precedent in our organization for people going from treasurer to president, and I had been on the executive committee for four years, so it made sense that I could do that. The Assembly of Delegates seemed to think that it was a good idea, and I did become president. I was the first person with a learning disability to become president of the organization, although others with disabilities were — and are — on the board.

I had sold my boat business and was winding that down, so that I was able to devote more time, practically full time, to being president of LDA. One of the things that I wanted to do as president was to strengthen the ties between the national organization and the state organizations, so during my two-year term as president I wanted to visit as many of the states as I possibly could. I was invited to come to more states than I could possibly do, because of conflicting schedules. However, I did go out many, many times.

What would happen was, I would be invited to visit a state during the time of their annual state conference. Sometimes I would be the keynote speaker for that conference, and also do a break-out session for them. Sometimes I would just do some break-out sessions and attend a local board meeting. Janet almost always went with me, and sometimes we would do sessions together. We had a program that we did on family and intimate relationships and the problems that people with learning disabilities and language difficulties have with them. Our presentations always generated lots of interaction and lots of compliments.

These trips gave us a look at learning disabilities and the needs from coast to coast. I was very surprised to hear the same stories that I had heard in Maine all across the country. Just as I had once assumed that only I had my kinds of problems, I had assumed that Maine's problems were unique to the state. I found out that learning disabilities are national, and now I can even believe that they are worldwide.

This was a very busy two years. We would be out for these conferences (they traditionally were done over a weekend), and we would get back into Maine on a Sunday night and the telephone would start ringing Monday morning and we'd be off and running again to do all kinds of things at the national level. It would happen sometimes that we would be out on weekends and work all week long and be out again, and I would come to realize that we'd worked for weeks and hadn't even had a day off.

One week I remember started with a state conference in Montana. I had also promised to be graduation speaker at Landmark East, a school for students with learning disabilities in Wolfville, Nova Scotia, at the end of the week. The only way to keep both engagements was to fly home from Montana, repack our bags, drive back to Portland and take the Prince of Fundy, a car ferry that goes from Portland to Yarmouth, Nova Scotia. It made the trip during the night. The next morning, we drove from Yarmouth to Wolfville and arrived in time to partici-pate in the graduation ceremony, the highlight of which was being piped into the hall by a Scottish bagpiper in full dress. We did take an extra day to explore Nova Scotia, and then returned from Yarmouth to Bar Harbor aboard the new high-speed ferry known as The Cat, a 50-mile-an-hour ride at sea.

Being based in Maine sometimes made winter travel a bit challenging. I remember one time, Janet and I were supposed to be going to our annual conference in Reno, preceded by an executive committee meeting which I was to run. The weather was bad and getting worse as we got on the plane in Bangor, heading for Boston. Almost at Logan Airport, we learned that the plane's landing gear wasn't working right, and the safest thing seemed to be to head back to Bangor. So we landed back where we started, still in the snow, and I spent hours in one line after another trying to get us on the next flight out. At last we decided so many flights were being canceled that there would be no plane for us, and we took the bus from Bangor to Boston. After a night in an airport hotel, and a fight with an airline to honor my tickets that had originated in Bangor, we got a flight to Reno and I arrived at the meeting I was supposed to be running – only four hours after it started.

Many other members of LDA's executive committee and board could tell similar stories. The board usually meets two or three times a year in addition to the national conference where we do most of our work, and the executive committee usually meets four or five times a year. The national conference is held in February and is moved all over the country to give people from different areas a chance to come. We always keep our fingers crossed that we won't get hit by a bad storm when we have a northern site. Many of the executive committee and board meetings are held in Chicago, since it's a central location (but not always of the best weather for traveling).

LDA conferences have an attendance of four to five thousand participants, a large hall of exhibitors, very appropriate keynote speakers and an extensive program to cover all aspects of learning disabilities, including education, parent advocacy, legal information, prevention through medical research, and the latest technology. We always enjoy a large awards banquet, where all in the field can come together for an evening of socialization. To accommodate such a large conference, we choose among the few hotels in the country large enough to provide the banquet hall, smaller program rooms, and number of bedrooms we need. Our organization has a program committee that selects all of the break-out and keynote speakers. A conference committee does all of the work of coordinating the conference, dealing with the hotel facility, publishing and distributing program booklets, and all of the hundreds of things that need to be done to make a conference come off smoothly and successfully. Our office staff also plays a very important role, keeping track of the speakers, organizing the program and doing the paperwork for registration and the program booklets. During my tenure as president, all these people, volunteers and staff, did a tremendous job, as they have been doing year after year.

Every now and then I get a glimpse of the importance of the work that we do. For example, at a conference in the Midwest, a woman caught up with me in the parking lot to thank me for being up-front and open about learning disabilities. She went on to say that she had had lots of problems with her children and family, and couldn't find out what was wrong, until one day a teacher suggested that she contact the local Learning Disabilities Association. She said that she started getting answers that were helping her family. Not only were her children having difficulties, so was her husband. And she ended the conversation by telling me that she had a 19-year-old son in jail.

According to LDA bylaws, the immediate past president stays on the executive committee for two years. As I write these paragraphs, I still have a lot of responsibilities on the executive committee, but I have been cutting back my work at the national level, and it is allowing me to do more of the local or state work that I did in the past. I don't have to do as much traveling, but I still get to work with all kinds of people with learning disabilities, and it keeps me involved and interested.

Social and Emotional Costs

As I began working on my own learning disabilities, I became aware of the fact that I had experienced lots of failures. These had gone back a long way. For me, they started when I started school. As I worked with other people, I could see that they had experienced lots of failure. For them, too, it went way back.

To do anything about these failures, we have to understand them and also be willing to face them. For instance, I don't know how many adults I've dealt with that would say, "Well, I do have a *little* reading problem," and if they got evaluated you would discover their reading was at third-grade level. A lot of the people that I have worked with have not been willing to face their disabilities, and consequently haven't been able to help themselves.

Most of us start this failure process when we start school, because school is so language-based or math-based that our difficulties show up right away. For most of us adults, there wasn't any understanding or any help in school. I find that even though I was in school starting in the late 1930s and through the 1940s, many people who went through school as late as in the 1970s and up into the 1980s had no help with schooling at all. But now the younger folks at least know they have learning disabilities, and there isn't just something weird and wrong with them. There are literally millions of people walking around who have no idea why they've had difficulty, or that it really isn't their fault that they've experienced so much lifetime failure.

Growing up with learning disabilities, we have consistently been told that we are failures in two areas where success is important: academically and socially. Laws say that we have to go to school, and many of us have experienced 14 or 15 or 16 years of school failure without any assistance. Many of us became high school dropouts. Even though we are only 10% of the population, we are 50% or more of high school dropouts.

Many of those dropouts eventually end up in GED (General Education Diploma) programs. I have seen some numbers on those programs that indicate as many as 70% or 75% may have learning disabilities. Many times, the learning disabilities aren't detected in those programs. Many of these students understand and know that they absolutely have to have an education if they're going to be successful in life, and they keep going back to school time after time and experiencing more failure. It frightens me that they don't get the kind of instruction that they need to be successful because, after a while, they're going to stop trying, and they may never make it.

We have discovered that about 60% of the adults in literacy programs (like those taught by Literacy Volunteers of America and similar organizations) have learning disabilities. Now we are beginning to train tutors in these literacy programs to use appropriate reading programs, and we're beginning to see more success.

I am 68 years old, and when I look back over 60 years to my first schooling, it still hurts. It is very easy for me to end up in tears as I think about it. I also can be moved to tears very easily if somebody tells me a story about a young boy failing in school. No matter how hard I tried, or how much I wanted to succeed, nothing ever worked. I became very isolated and lonely. I didn't have any friends, and the teacher was mad at me. I didn't know what was going to happen next, but I was pretty sure it wasn't going to be good. So as a first grader, what did I do with all these troubles and feelings? I simply shut down. I did what I could to become invisible and stay out of trouble. If I got in trouble, I simply knew that the end of the day would come, that somehow or another it would get over with. I became very quiet and just waited for the time to pass.

I must have been very good at withdrawing, because I don't have any memory now of the second, third, or fourth grades. By the time I got to high school, it was pretty well established how I was to operate, which was not to make any waves, not to get in any arguments, not to cause any trouble, and quietly do what I had to do to get by. When I got to high school, I was experiencing classes that I could succeed in, such as algebra and math and science, but I still didn't participate in class discussions, ask any questions of the instructor; I just quietly listened and did the best I could. In the areas that I had a natural ability in, I did learn and was successful in them. The same thing was true when I went to college. I disappeared in the back row, with all the S's, and the instructor never heard from me for the rest of the semester. Some instructors never even got to know my name or know anything about me.

By the time I became an adult, I had grown myself a thick shell. There wasn't anything you could say to me or do to me that would make me mad or upset or get me going in any way. This whole thing might have worked better if I could have been selective and shut down only the feelings that were giving me a bad time. However, that doesn't seem to be the way it works. If we shut down one thing, we shut down everything. And with that go the feelings of joy, happiness, love and the kinds of things that we don't want to lose. So in the end, it wasn't the best way to go.

On top of all this, I discovered that all of the troubles I had were still there, waiting on a back burner to erupt sometime for me. This happened 15 years ago when I started investigating my own learning disabilities and trying to understand what had happened and why. All of a sudden, there were lots of tears, pain and fears that I had to deal with. This is 15 years later, and there is no way that I would want to go back to doing business the way I used to. I now can get angry on occasion, I can have some tears over the learning disabilities business, I have a lot stronger feelings for my wife and my family and for those that I work with in the learning disabilities field. And on occasion, I

70

get a glimpse of peace.

My story is one of becoming passive and withdrawn. That's the way it affected me, and a lot of the people I work with have had similar experiences. However, there are other experiences that I would like to share.

One of them is that an awful lot of the people that I have worked with tell me stories about becoming a class clown. I think that these tend to be people that are very verbal, but still have language troubles, particularly written language difficulties and comprehension difficulties. Their coping mechanism was to be very popular in the class, telling jokes and doing funny things and keeping the rest of the class laughing and having a good time. Lots of times they could even get the teachers to participate. If they did a good job, they could delay their work long enough so that a spelling test wouldn't be given that day, or some reading wouldn't have to be done. These students tended to fit in better and not have as many social problems. The teachers, I think, were not as angry with them, because of the humor and the fun that everybody seemed to have in the classes. However, they did manage to disrupt the classes and keep a lot of the work from being done; and eventually, their lack of ability to do schoolwork would catch up with them.

Another thing that happens is that students become angry over their frustration and school failures and develop behavioral problems. This is very prevalent, and I hear stories about fights breaking out, students doing bizarre things that disrupt the school, and the principal coming down to the school room lots of times to straighten out difficulties. When I was in school, kids who acted like that got a good licking and got sent home. Now, these folks are more likely to get services through the school's special education program, because they are right in the teacher's face lots of times with problems, and the teachers recognize the behavioral difficulties more often than they do the language or math difficulties. They're willing to set up programs to handle discipline problems because they need to do that for their own survival.

Because we're in trouble with the teacher, we will usually have trouble with the other kids in the class. The kids know that the teacher's impatient with us and unhappy with us. It's apparent that there's something wrong, and we also think that there's something wrong, because we don't understand what's happening. The other kids tend to not want to have anything to do with us or to play with us or to interact with us socially at all. So not only do we miss out on our education, we become isolated. Some of us experience depression. Many of us need professional counseling to deal with these social problems that start when we are in school.

Most of us who have learning disabilities have problems in doing things appropriately. These difficulties are considered to be executive function issues. We can't get our schoolwork done; as adults, we can't get our livelihood work done. We procrastinate. We have trouble understanding social messages. These areas are all difficult to deal with. I think that there hasn't been much research done on this area, and it is an area that has many implications for our success. I'm hoping that, in the future, studies will be directed in this area.

I was working with a young man, and I asked him if he had a steady girlfriend. His answer was no, he didn't, because he had tried that and he got into too much difficulty — he couldn't remember to call when he was supposed to, and one time he didn't even pick her up when he was supposed to. So he was always in a hassle and had all kinds of trouble, and he said, "I just can't handle it and I don't even try any more."

I was recently talking on the phone with a father that had a teenage son with all kinds of difficulties in school. I was explaining to him about short-term memory problems and how it involved so much of school work. I had been saying that a student has to remember to get his assignment to do his homework at night. Then he has to bring the assignment and the books he needs home. Then he has to remember after dinner to do the homework. Then the next morning he has to remember to take the assignment back to school. Finally, he has to remember to pass it in in class. There's an awful lot of memory work to each of these steps. The father found this story interesting, because, he told me, his son had done a special assignment to get through a course in which he had difficulty. The boy had been very interested in it, and the instructor said that he had been back to talk with him two or three times about the assignment. He finally got it all ready and was supposed to pass it in the next day at school, and he had gone off to a sports meet and forgotten to turn it in. Everybody was thinking how irresponsible he had been, and assumed he was not interested enough to think about turning his report in; but it really was a short-term memory problem. So that father knew exactly what I was talking about; it will be the parents' — and the son's — responsibility to find some way for the boy to keep track of all these different things.

One adult that I worked with said that he was spiteful, and that was the reason that he didn't do his work in school and didn't succeed. I tried to explain to him that somebody had probably told that to him, and that the reason that he really couldn't do the work was because he didn't have the abilities in those areas. He would talk more about it all, and we'd have more discussion, and he'd come back to some other part of it, and he'd say, "Well, don't you think that's spiteful?"

I would keep trying to explain to him that I didn't, that a lot of people had these same kinds of problems, and that his failure was because he couldn't do the work, not because he didn't want to do the work. I worked with him for several hours, because he had to understand that he wasn't spiteful before he could understand his real problems and help himself. He was using being spiteful as a block, to avoid making changes that might be painful and frightening. It was impossible to get him to understand that his difficulties weren't because he was spiteful.

He was working for an electronics company with an inner-city plant in Boston. He had become so valuable to the company that, even though he couldn't get to work on time and was having difficulties keeping his schedule (because of executive-function problems), finally the company said that it would be okay for him to work his eight hours any time during the day he wanted. And he said that every day he intended to get up and go to work at eight or nine o'clock the next morning, and do his work and come home at a regular time. But, he said, day after day he wouldn't get in to work until six or seven o'clock in the evening, and he would end his eight-hour shift in the wee hours of the morning. Because he couldn't handle an automobile, partly because he lived in the city, he was using a bicycle to go back and forth to work, and he ended up riding through some of the real rough parts of Boston at two or three o'clock in the morning to get home after work. He was very intelligent and had lots of good marketable skills, but he hadn't recognized that, and he probably still hasn't. I hope that he is still making out all right, riding his bicycle at two o'clock in the morning in Boston.

I remember one young man I worked with who had been misdiagnosed as being MR (mentally retarded) instead of LD. It happened that his older brother had been evaluated for learning disabilities, and somehow his brother's age had ended up on his evaluation. Because of that discrepancy, he wasn't functioning at the right age level, and automatically it made his evaluation look as though he was mentally retarded. His nightmare was that he had to go to school on the "dummy bus," and he absolutely hated that, and he was in the wrong program at school, and his life was just absolutely miserable. He eventually did get reevaluated and was found to have learning disabilities, and it changed his whole life. He was very, very grateful to get more appropriate help once he was reevaluated.

This kid was in a group of kids who had been brought together in a school for a support group type of experience. We brought this group to one of our state conferences, and they told their stories about going to school and having learning disabilities. It was so emotional for them that they would sometimes break right down and cry as they told what had happened. It had been all worked out so that sometimes when one of them would be crying so hard that he or she wouldn't be able to continue, another one would take over; when the one that was having problems recovered enough, he'd come back and tell the rest of his story. It was a very emotional thing to watch these kids who had had so much pain at school share it with others.

These kids don't want to be excluded, they don't want to be outsiders, they want to be just regular kids like all the others. They want to be successful in school, they want to learn to read, but these things are just so difficult for them to achieve.

As a group, those of us with learning disabilities tend to have very poor self-esteem. We get depressed and sometimes very angry. In general, we end up feeling like complete outsiders. Even though we might have skills in some areas other than language or math, we tend to discount our abilities in those areas, because we think if there's anything that we can do, it's not too difficult, and anybody could do it. Which of course is not true; we all have skills that are very valuable. If people with leaning disabilities recognize their abilities, they realize that they can earn their living, find things they like to do and gain respect from others, all of which will improve their self-esteem.

Many times, parents can be just as impatient as teachers. This is kind of a double problem for a lot of people, because they don't get any support anywhere. One of the questions that I sometimes ask in support group work is, "Where were your parents when all of these problems were going on at school?" Some people are very angry over the fact that their parents didn't understand and didn't help. On the other hand, there are lots of instances where parents did try and did want to help, but couldn't find any way to do it. For those parents, their adult children found that quite acceptable, and appreciated the effort anyway, and the anger wasn't there.

75

Learning disabilities and corrections

I first started working with young people with learning disabilities in the early 1960s, when my family and I lived in Westborough, Massachusetts, only then I didn't understand what the problems were or know what I could do to help. As a community project, I started doing volunteer work at Lyman School for Boys, a juvenile correction facility run by the Division of Youth Services of the Commonwealth of Massachusetts.

The school was located on the top of a ridge, with lots of open space. The buildings were very old and brick, typical state-institution-type architecture. The kids lived in what were called cottages; however, they looked to me more like old, ominous brick dormitories. These "cottages" were placed around a green, like a village green. There was a separate cafeteria, gymnasium, and school. It also had been a farm school, so there were lots of barns and storage buildings. There were several hundred acres to the whole school, which gave it lots of wooded land plus lots of open fields. There was an administration building and there were several separate houses for staff. The whole thing was laid out very nicely as a typical campus — a good place for kids, with lots of trees and lots of mowed lawns. It also was a very open campus — no fences or anything that would restrict anybody if they wanted to leave. Not many boys ran away, though occasionally one did.

My volunteer job entailed going once a week to the school and spending some time with the kids. We played basketball, played ping-pong, just generally visited. It was, I think, a very good thing for the kids in there to have some association with people on the outside. They didn't have that opportunity unless somebody came in.

After a while, I could see that these kids didn't have enough to do. They did have a school, but they didn't have anything for vocational education. I thought this would be a real good project, and it was the kind of thing that interested me. So one night at a meeting, I suggested that it would be nice to set up a vocational education program for some of these kids. Everybody agreed that it would be a wonderful idea, and asked if I would do it.

I started working with Bob Brown, a chaplain at Lyman School. One of the first things we decided was that these kids were all interested in automobiles, just like any kids are, and they would have a natural interest and it would be a very good place to do some vocational work. We called the class the auto mechanics class, and started in. We made arrangements to have a shop to work in, and the first students were selected. We worked with the older students, 15 through 17 years old. They had to have an interest in auto mechanics, and they all had to be volunteers.

I arrived at the school the first night, and I took my mechanic's tool chest in. At the shop, the kids were there waiting for me — and the shop was locked; I couldn't get in. That first night, we had our class, just the same; we went all over my tool box and talked about the names of the tools and what they were used for. The kids had lots of questions about automobiles and engines. So, in spite of not getting into the shop, we did have a lesson and it did go okay. The kids learned something about auto mechanics, and I started to learn a little bit about working with a state institution. The kids were asking questions about was I going to come back again and was it going to continue, and I could see from their questions that they weren't used to things being ongoing and continuous. They were pretty suspicious that this might be just a one-time thing. I could see that they had a real need for doing something week after week, and that probably they had been disappointed over these things many times in their lives. I came away that night with a determination that if I was going to do this, it was going to be done every single week. And it was, for 10 years.

I did get access to the shop worked out. In this garage, there was a 30-year old Ford fire truck. I don't think it had been moved for years. The odometer had 300 miles on it, so it was all like brand new. One of our projects was to keep this fire truck up. We would run it every few weeks and take it out around the campus. This gave the kids a chance to ride on the truck. They thought it was great sport, and they started taking responsibility for maintaining it and keeping it going well.

There were two Farmall M tractors, left over from when Lyman School was a farm school, that were still used for odd jobs. We started servicing them. Slowly the staff began to understand that we were there to stay, and we were doing some work, and it was helping them out, too.

After a few months, the school cleared out a small three-bay garage that was to be used for the auto mechanics class exclusively. This gave us a place where we could have some equipment and leave it and have some vehicles that we were working on kept secure. Then we started working on vehicles for the school. We started doing tune-ups, oil changes, and general service for several of the cars that the school used.

After a while, we discovered in the basement of the cafeteria a whole bunch of auto repair work equipment that had been bought years ago to do a vocational class, just like we were doing. There was an automobile lift, tire-changing equipment, all kinds of things that were going to be just great. With this discovery, the school agreed to make a new shop, which was going to be much bigger, in an unused part of the steam plant. It required quite a lot of work; they had to put in a new overhead door and install all of the equipment, but they did this. So after a while, we moved into a nice brand-new shop with lots of new equipment. This wouldn't have happened if Bob Brown hadn't been very interested and done a lot of work with the school to make it all happen. Bob, at about this point, became one of the volunteer instructors in the course.

With the new space and the new equipment, we could do a lot more work, and we expanded the whole project to include other volunteer instructors. There were times that we had five or six instructors and we ran the classes two nights a week. We could do almost all of the mechanical work for the whole school. This included working on maintenance trucks, lawn equipment and several vehicles that were used by the school to move the students around.

One of the things the school wanted was a bus so that they could take groups of kids to various events. They didn't have any funds to buy a bus. Because of my experience in truck sales, I managed to get hold of a used school bus. It was quite used, but that was okay, because the school had funds for repair, and we went right through the bus and rebuilt it. It gave the school another vehicle to use, and gave us more work to do.

The whole project turned out to be very successful, and it ran until the school closed, when the Commonwealth began contracting out juvenile correctional services to private providers. I liked the kids, and I enjoyed doing the work; if that hadn't been so, I never would have done it for 10 years. But it was always a mystery to me as to why it had worked so well. This was all done before I knew anything about learning disabilities or dyslexia, or knew that I had those conditions. As I began to learn about learning disabilities, I began to understand how that project at Lyman School had worked. The reason was that these kids had learning disabilities or dyslexia, just as I did; and they had natural mechanical abilities and interest, just as I did.

Even back when I was running the program, I could see that these kids were a lot like I was. I kept asking myself, "Why are these kids on the inside while I'm on the outside?"

I taught these kids the way that I learn, and that was the exact way to do it. I had a stripped-down automobile. All the sheet metal was off it; the only thing that was left was the running gear, frame, motor, transmission and drive line. I would stand by the motor with a bunch of kids around so that they could all see and start naming off the various parts. I'd say, "This is the water pump," and talk about the water pump and explain what it does and why. Then I'd go on to the distributor and the carburetor and all the various parts of the engine, and name and describe the use of each part. During these discussions, the kids and I would often actually have our hands on the part we were talking about. I didn't know it at the time, but

79

using our tactile sense is one part of what is called multi-sensory teaching, which is exactly what many people with learning disabilities need.

Sometimes I'd see the kids back over there by the car in groups of two or three, and they would be doing exactly the same thing I had done. They'd put their hand on something, and you could see that they were trying to bring up what it was called. In the group, there would probably be somebody who would remember that this is the carburetor, this is the distributor, and they would learn that way. Once in a while, they'd have to come and ask me about a particular name, but they were very interested in getting their vocabulary and knowing what all the things were so that they could talk about it.

This stripped-down car was in working condition. I did take the drive line out of it, so that we wouldn't have an accident with the darn thing, but I could start it by putting a fuel line into a gas can and using a battery as a jumper. Once the kids understood theoretically how everything worked together to make the car run, I would start it, so the kids could see and hear and smell that it really did work.

Servicing the school vehicles was another wonderful teaching tool. I would break the class up into small groups, depending on how many I had and how many instructors there were — maybe three, four, or five people to a group — and assign each group a particular job. One of them might be changing oil in a vehicle and doing a grease job, another one tuning a vehicle up, or changing tires, or doing muffler work, or whatever. I'd tell them how to do the job, and they were trained to go as far as they could go; if they had any questions or a problem, they were to stop. I would go from one group to another during the course of the evening, to check up on them and see if they had problems. If they did, we'd have a discussion about how they needed to solve the problem, and they would start going again. It worked out very well. I could take a group of 15 or 20 and keep them busy for a whole evening.

I had things like a collection of carburetors (this was back in the days before fuel injection). I not only taught them how to take a carburetor apart, to have a little box to put all the parts in so that nothing would get lost, to keep your bench cleaned up so that you could keep track of things and not get dirt in it, and to be careful; I also taught them what all the parts were for and what they did and how they worked. So, as we took one apart, we could talk about all of the different jets and the float valve and accelerator pump and how each played a part in how the automobile worked. They were allowed to take them apart and put them back together. I had a whole collection, and some of them were very simple single-barrel carburetors. If you got really good and didn't lose any parts, you got to take apart the big four-barrel Holly.

We had both acetylene and arc welding, and everybody had a chance at this. Everybody ran a burning torch, and everybody welded with the arc welder. This was difficult for some, and some did it very naturally and easily — they could strike an arc without assistance and hold an arc well. When I found these students who had real natural abilities, I'd share that with them afterwards, when the whole class wasn't there. Even though I didn't know then about learning disabilities, I knew about failure, and I knew that these kids needed to know they could do something well and have their self-esteem strengthened. Other kids could hardly do it at all, and I'd have to put my hand right over their hand and strike the arc. But they got the feel for it, and learned what it was and the vocabulary involved, and also the safety precautions that anybody needs to observe in doing this kind of work.

The kids were responsible for doing everything in the shop. They swept up at night when we were done, they cleaned up the tools and put them all away, and they really seemed to enjoy that as part of their whole evening. There was never a problem in getting people to participate completely in everything we did.

Sometimes, when we got our work done, if it was early enough, we'd all go down to the local ice cream stand and they could have an ice cream or a cold drink. You would think that this wouldn't be a difficult thing to do, but I discovered right away that it was a problem for the kids. They were very self-conscious about their clothing; they were wearing state-issued clothes that had been made elsewhere in the correctional system, and they weren't as stylish as what the kids on the street would be wearing. They worried about that a lot. They especially worried there might be girls there, who would see them not looking their best; and there always were.

When I first started doing this, some of the kids would say they hadn't been off the school grounds for six months or a year, so they weren't used to being on the outside and it really scared them. I learned not to talk about it ahead of time; what I would do, on one of those evenings when it was possible to have a few minutes to go out, was just say, "All right, get in the car and we're going to go have an ice cream." Before they knew what had happened to them, they'd be standing in line at the ice cream place.

Another thing I used to do in the evenings was to run a driver education program. Many times, people would give me automobiles to use in the auto mechanics class. Some of them were in running condition when we got them; for others, it didn't take us much work to get them running. I used them to teach the kids how to drive. The school had huge grounds and old fields and roads down in back that we could use. I would fill the car up with four or five kids and get somebody behind the wheel. They'd start driving and practicing and talking about it, and it was something that the kids were all just as excited about doing as they could be. Like all kids, they wanted to know how to drive an automobile.

All of these things that I did, I certainly didn't keep as a secret from the school. However, I didn't talk with them a lot about it, either. I learned early on that it was very difficult for the institution to give me permission to do certain things that I wanted to do. On the other hand, the same institution couldn't say no, either. So I managed to get a lot of work done, and it worked out really well with the kids. Fortunately, we didn't have any difficulties with anything — nobody got hurt, we did no major property damage, and not too many rules were broken.

I had an arrangement with the school that I didn't want to know anything about the background of the kids or why they were there, unless it was a condition that I had to know. For example, some of the kids were fire-setters and some were real fighters; I needed to know about those things ahead of time, so that I'd be aware. I also had to be aware of any medical conditions that might need attention.

However, I did work with the staff on some of the kids. For instance, one of the things that they used to do from time to time was a case study on a particular student. If he happened to be in my class, I'd participate. We would all sit around and go over a particular set of records and get to understand what all of the background was and why he was there, and what the family situation was. It was to get people trained as to what these kids were really like and where they were coming from. I found it very educational. However, it was also very disturbing, because it was unbelievable, some of the abusive backgrounds that these kids had come from. A lot of things that we were dealing with were very grim.

I think that when you get into those kinds of circumstances, oftentimes to relieve the pressure you use a little humor to help life along. I did end up with a very good relationship with the counselors and other staff members. I took the stance with the counselors that counseling was just barely tolerable, and that they needed to get out from behind their desks into the real world. They would start pulling tricks on me to get even. They would sometimes have kids they couldn't figure out or didn't know what to do with or were having hard luck with. The first thing that they would do was put them in my auto mechanics class. Then after a few weeks they'd ask me what I thought about so-and-so. Usually, I would have something to say. But it didn't come about because I was any smarter than they were; it would happen that I'd watched the student work with his peers, and I could make some pretty good observations.

One time, they had a 15-year-old boy who was doing weight lifting. He was jerking 225 pounds, and he was so big and strong that some of the staff were actually frightened of him. In addition, his behavior was unpredictable and close to unacceptable, but never quite over the line. He delighted in keeping staff members confused and worried, and in laughing at them when he did something unexpected. So they did tell me about this kid, before they put him in my class. And they were right – he was disruptive, and he caused all kinds of problems in the class. It was so bad, he drove one of my volunteers right out of the program.

Then one night, I came to realize that this kid was really messing with my mind. I never knew where he was coming from or what he was going to do next. And he was having a ball doing it. Of course, he did have an advantage – the only thing he had on his mind was toying with me, and I was trying to run a mechanics class, which was getting difficult.

So I reported back to the counselors that this kid was extremely smart. They said, "What we need to do is give him an IQ test." He came back with a score of 140. We all got together for a discussion of what was going to happen with this whole situation. My comment was, "You're simply just going to tell him."

We got into a long discussion of how to tell him all of this. Everybody decided that probably it would work best if I told him. Of course, they were all getting a good chuckle out of this, because they knew how hard it was going to be.

The next week, I asked the kid to stay for a few minutes after class, because I wanted to talk to him. After all the other kids had gone, I asked him, "Do you remember that you've had some testing done recently?"

He said, "Yes."

I said, "Do you know why that was?"

He didn't know. I told him that it was to test his general intelligence, and that the results had come back. I told him exactly what the number was: 140.

Of course, he didn't know what that meant. I started to explain to him that he was probably the brightest kid that I'd ever had in my auto mechanics class, and that he could do anything he wanted to, and go anywhere he wanted, and all of that kind of good stuff. It didn't register with him at all; he had no idea what I was really talking about. I would try another approach and that wouldn't work either. So, finally, I looked the kid right in the eye, and I said, "You're smarter than I am." And he kind of froze. He got it.

I did have a little talk with him about what he was doing with his intelligence, and that probably he could use it in other ways and help himself a lot more. He was bright, and he caught on real fast. He turned into my assistant and became very helpful in the class with the other kids. The staff was able to deal with him much better, and he went on to do some very positive things at school.

All of these kids I dealt with learned enough about mechanics so that they were at a job entry level and could have gone to work in a filling station or garage, not as full-fledged mechanics, but as able to begin and at least become employed. But I found in checking on my kids that their recidivism rate was not one bit better than the school as a whole. This was always a mystery to me. Now I know that I had taught them to do auto mechanics work, but I hadn't addressed any of their needs as far as their disabilities were concerned. As I look back on all of this, I wish I could go back and do it over again and address all of their needs. I'll bet that their recidivism rate would be a lot better.

After a couple of years, I had a class that I thought was doing very well. I'd had most of the students for several months, and they were learning well, and I thought it would be a wonderful opportunity to start in with a sit-down class for these students, so that they weren't always just working on vehicles. The school thought it would be a good idea. They bought me a whole set of wonderful textbooks to use — they were well illustrated, they had pictures and drawings and I thought were perfect books to be used for this class. I told the kids about what we going to do, and I distributed the brand-new textbooks, and the very first week that we tried to have a sit-down class, it didn't work at all. The students thought that I had really betrayed them, they got angry over the whole deal, and they weren't cooperative and didn't want anything to do with having a regular sit-down class. That was pretty hard for me then to understand the reasoning behind it, but they just hadn't had any kind of success in school and with books, and they weren't going to go in that direction. I did run that class for two weeks, but it wasn't to be. I was in and out of that project very quickly, because that wasn't the kind of thing that those kids needed. They needed to be on their feet actually doing the work with vehicles and in the shop.

Since I have learned more about education, I have discovered that my teaching techniques for the kids were all very implicit. That was the way that I had learned, and that was the way that I was teaching the students; and it happened that that was exactly the way that they needed. What I was specifically doing was giving them the opportunity; they had displayed the interest. We provided a shop for them to work in, the tools to use and the projects for them to get involved with.

What I was doing at Lyman School turns out to be a perfect example of how to teach implicitly. The students had natural abilities in the subject, and the instructor did, too, and had also learned implicitly, so the whole system worked very nicely.

The other part of the story is that if we have to learn something in an area we don't have natural abilities in, we need direct, explicit instruction. For me, that area is language. The only way that I can learn language is with explicit instruction. And the same would be true for most of those kids that I was dealing with at Lyman School.

Dr. Coughlan, who was the director of all of the youth corrections programs for the State of Massachusetts, got interested in the shop project we had at Lyman School. He started coming by every two or three months while the shop was in use to see what was going on and how it was being run. After a few visits, he started coming by me quietly and asking about all of the other volunteers that were working in the shop, who they were and what their experience was and a little bit of history on them. He'd go along and visit with them a little bit and introduce himself and thank them for participating in the shop. After a little while, it came to me that Dr. Coughlan didn't understand that I was a volunteer; he had mistaken me as being part of the school staff. This pleased me; I was actually flattered to think that he figured I was part of his staff. When I reported this to the staff at the school, they became very concerned that he had misinterpreted what was happening in the shop and wanted to correct the situation. I told them no, we weren't going to do that, we were going to leave it just as it was, and I had a good time running a charade for several years about who was a volunteer and who was staff in the shop. As it turned out, Dr. Coughlan never did discover that I wasn't staff.

Since I've been in the learning disabilities field, I have discovered that the incidence of learning disabilities among prison populations is unbelievably high, and Janet and I have done some work in this area. The incidence of learning disabilities in juvenile corrections may be as high as 60 or 70 percent, depending on who is included in the count. It is also very high among adult offenders. Back when I was teaching at Lyman School, we sometimes visited at Walpole State Prison. When we mixed with the population and they discovered that we were from Lyman School, it was like old home day – everybody wanted to know if such-and-such an instructor was still there, or a cottage master, and what was happening, and had all kinds if questions. So I know that juvenile corrections is very closely linked to adult corrections, and I suspect the numbers may be very similar.

I have found that there seems to be very little knowledge about learning disabilities in corrections, among both prison populations and service providers. However, the people I've worked with have been very interested and very receptive to the kinds of things that will help people with learning disabilities. One of the things that I have done is spend some time working with Maine juvenile parole officers, and they have been very interested. It was a lot of information that they didn't know, but when I started talking about it, they could see how it fitted with many of the people they were working with. Working for the Learning Disabilities Association of Maine, Janet and I also did training for tutors in adult corrections. This was very helpful in getting some appropriate types of reading programs for inmates who couldn't read.

Janet and I had the opportunity to present in the state women's correctional unit in Montana, and had a very good session. The women were particularly interested in the social and emotional issues surrounding learning disabilities. It helped those there to understand what had happened to them and gave them a chance to learn more about some of their difficulties. We also presented in the state women's correctional unit in Iowa. As a result, a new reading program was instituted in that particular unit, and now I understand that it has been expanded and is in a second unit. So these things can help, once people start understanding what the difficulties are and some ways to cope with them. I find that in corrections there are tremendous needs for knowledge, information, and support in the areas of learning disabilities. These folks desperately need help, and this is an area that is in need of all kinds of work.

Learning disabilities and substance abuse

In the late 1980s, the director of the substance abuse program at Mid-Maine Medical Center (now MaineGeneral Medical Center) in Waterville called me about learning disabilities. He said that he thought that a lot of their clients had learning disabilities. My immediate response was that a lot of the people that I am working with have substance abuse issues. After a long discussion, we put together a plan to introduce learning disabilities to the hospital staff, counselors and doctors involved with the program.

This program was a 28-day residency program in a hospital setting. This means the person in charge on the floor was a nurse, not a counselor. There actually were two different programs, one for adolescents and the other for adults. These programs were well established and had been in existence for some years. We planned for me to visit with each program once a month.

To start the program, I did an in-service training program for all of the staff, including doctors, nurses, counselors, some volunteers, and some other interested hospital personnel. We all gathered in a large conference room, 50 or 60 people. I explained what learning disabilities are, how we tend to have a lot of school failures, social failures, and work-related failures. I also gave them lots of suggestions about what can be done to help people with learning disabilities, and talked about the necessity for those people around people with learning disabilities to understand and help with the condition, not to criticize because of it. I had lots and lots of questions from the staff; we had a wonderful, open discussion about the possibilities of working with learning disabilities. The session lasted nearly two hours. It was also videotaped; this videotape was used by the hospital for years as part of the training process for new personnel that were going to be involved in treatment.

I very quickly moved into meeting with the clients in the programs. There was some nervousness about somebody new who wasn't really tried or understood coming into the programs, so one of the doctors accompanied me in some of the first sessions. I met with the clients in a conference room right on the floor of the hospital, where they lived and worked. We sat in a circle, which was very comfortable for me, because that is the way I had been conducting support group meetings, and it was the way that they do a lot of group counseling. The number in a group ranged from six to twelve, men and women, and from all walks of life. I would share with them some of my difficulties in school and how I had struggled to get my education, and also a lot of the social problems that arise for anyone that has communication problems. I was amazed at how fast they identified with the things that I had to say. They had already been trained, in the program, to deal with personal issues and feelings, so they very quickly could address learning disabilities issues if they had them.

I later kept track of the incidence, and found, anecdotally, that in this substance abuse program, about 70% of the adults and about 50% of the adolescents had a learning disability, or ADHD (hyperactivity), or both. A very high percentage also had math disability and the executive-function types of problems that we all tend to have.

The math disability was more prevalent than I had expected. I soon discovered that the counselors were math-disabled. They had excellent language abilities, which were necessary for them to communicate and keep records, which was what their job was all about. They also had very good interpersonal abilities, which was a perfect setup for a good counselor. They started telling me their stories about difficulties with math. Please keep in mind that most counselors in substance abuse treatment have been through the program and are themselves recovering.

One counselor told me, after a session one night, that she had been a straight-A student in school. School was interesting, fun and exciting for her. I knew her to be a very conscientious, hard-working person, and she took great pride in being a top student. When she got into high school and started to take algebra, she just simply could not do it. Her instructor said that she was a very bright girl and that if she would try and pay attention, she'd be able to do the algebra also. Because nobody in the situation understood anything about math disability, this woman floundered terribly in high school and just barely graduated, with no hope of going on to college or any other kind of education. She was in tears telling me this story, and she was just finding out that her difficulty had a name and could be understood, and that there were many things to do to help it.

Another counselor shared his story, which was very similar. He had done well in school until he got into high school and couldn't do algebra or trigonometry. He liked sports and was playing varsity football. Even though he was having trouble in math, his success in sports kept him going; he had friends and was doing all right socially because of the sports. However, eventually he failed math. Because school policy required athletes to be passing all their courses, he was kicked off the football team — a typical example of a school taking away from a student what he could do because of what he couldn't do. Losing football changed his whole life. He started running with a different group of friends and, he said, no fault from them, but he started drinking and his life went downhill. He did eventually graduate from college with a bachelor of science degree, and went into counseling. After learning about his math disability and understanding that he was bright in lots of other areas, he went back to school and got a master's degree with straight A's.

During my five years working in substance abuse treatment, I estimate that I dealt with about 100 different counselors. Out of that 100 counselors, I think there was only one woman that I did not consider math-disabled. This is very anecdotal; I don't know if it would be true of another program, but I feel that it would probably be so. These counselors were wonderful working with clients; they also took an interest in what I was doing, they had suggestions for ways that I could work better with clients, but they were math-disabled, and they didn't know it.

Every session I ever did in substance abuse treatment was interesting. I learned that the clients were interested in what we had to say, and even though it was a one-time deal for me, the counselors would be following up afterwards any new material or any new directions that the clients might need to go in. The counselors were telling me that, days after I'd had a session, the clients would still be talking about what it was that they needed to deal with out of that session.

One of the sessions stands out in my mind. In some ways, it was a lot like all of the sessions that I did. However, this one dealt with a lot of different issues that are important, and I would like to share this session in detail, so that you can see how they work.

There were about 10 clients, and Martha was there that night to co-facilitate. Martha was a minister in my church who, I discovered, had learning disabilities. She became very interested in the work that I was doing, and helped co-facilitate a lot of my group work. Martha and I were explaining about our disabilities and how they had affected us, and we went on and did the routine about what our abilities are. People were participating and asking good questions and things were going along very normally.

But I became aware that the fellow that was sitting on my immediate left wasn't participating. From the way that he was struggling with his verbal expression, I guessed that he had a learning disability. So when it became time for everybody to pick out a couple of areas that they are good in and like and that work well for them, and a couple of areas that they struggle with and they don't like and it just doesn't work, I started around the circle on the opposite side from the man that was having his verbal expression problems. My thinking was that the others in the group would model what he needed to do when it came his turn. I thought listening to them would help him.

When we got around the circle (and it takes quite a while to do this with each person), eventually it was his turn, and I asked him what areas worked for him and what he liked to do. His immediate reply was, "There isn't anything that I can do. I've tried, and just nothing works for me."

When people get stuck like this, I usually start asking them questions about various things, such as, "When you were in school, what was your favorite subject?" or "What was the one that you disliked most?" Sometimes you get insight from that.

But his answer was always "No, there isn't anything I can do," or "I couldn't do anything in school." Every time I mentioned something, his response was always the same.

Finally I asked him what he had done to earn his living. He

was a man in his 50s, probably, so that he had to have done something. His reply was, "I was a professional musician. I played the trumpet."

"Wow! You're a professional musician? You're really talented and you've got something that is very special."

He hadn't thought of that or seen that or even thought about it as being special!

We talked a bit about having musical ability being special, and the fact that he had earned his living with it indicating that he was very gifted in the area of music, so that he did have an unusual talent. I thought he was beginning to catch on a little bit that there was something he was good at.

I had discovered, working with these folks with talents in music or other areas, but particularly in music, that if they have these natural abilities, they can pick up an instrument and play it almost without instruction. They remember music in their head and don't have to even have sheet music to go by, because they've got it all in their mind and can play it and do wonderful, interesting things. So I asked him if he played any other instrument besides the trumpet.

His answer was, "No, I don't play anything else, except all of the horns."

It was such a ridiculous downer that all of us in the group laughed, including me; we just couldn't help it. In a support group meeting you never laugh at anybody, but we all had.

Martha immediately said to the man, "Do you know why we have laughed?"

He ended up with a very bewildered, pained expression on his face, and he had absolutely no idea why the laughter had occurred. I can still see him; he was hurting immensely, and he was half risen up out of his chair, and he would have liked to have run out of the place, but he just couldn't.

Martha said, "We all need to tell you why we laughed."

I said, "That's exactly right, and I'll go first."

I explained to him that I couldn't play an instrument of any kind, but I would like to, and the fact that he could play all of the horns, and didn't see that as special, just struck me as funny, and I couldn't help but laugh. We went all the way around the circle, and every single person there shared with him how it had affected them, and why they had laughed.

After we had that squared away, I spent some time with him to find out where he was with the horns and what he had done. He said that he loved the horns, and he had had a whole collection of every one of them. When he started drinking, the horns all got sold for drink, and they were all gone.

After a little bit, I suggested to him that now that he was in a recovery program, there was a good chance that he could get back to the horns if he wanted to. If I read the body language right, that was a thought that hadn't even crossed his mind yet.

This was just a perfect example of what happens when we experience extreme school failure. We use that school success so many times as a measure of our intelligence; when we can't succeed in school, we think that we're real dumb, and when other things come along that we can do, we discount them, thinking "Anybody can do it" or "That's nothing special; because I'm so dumb, if I can do it, anybody can."

When things like this came out in the meetings, I would always share them with the counselors, so that they could follow up. I wasn't going to be able to follow up, but he would have some help with it.

I have to admit that I was really touched by this man, by his openness and his honesty, but particularly for his pain. Afterwards, I started wondering how much a used trumpet would cost, and thinking how nice it would be to take one in to the unit. I even drove by the pawn shop. But the more I thought about it, it seemed to me that he had drunk up all his horns, and it was in his best interest, if he was going to have a horn again, to do it on his own.

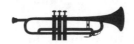

Solutions for Adults
and Young Adults

Those of us who have learning disabilities are disabled in different ways. I can't tell anybody how to solve their problems, because we all have to work up our own system for our particular combination of disabilities. We not only have to understand our disabilities, we also have to understand our abilities, because we must learn to use our abilities to help us in the areas of our disabilities. I offer some of the ideas that have worked for me, and also the methods that I went through to determine what would help.

When I was in my early 50s, I knew that I couldn't read effectively, I couldn't spell, I couldn't write, and I had all kinds of oral expression problems. I had never heard about learning disabilities or dyslexia, and I also had never met anybody who said that they had these kinds of difficulties. I thought I was the only person in the world with these language problems. I thought there was something really wrong with me, that I was kind of weird, and I was ashamed of all these differences, and I ended up with a dark secret about it all, which really was a block toward getting any help. This is the same spot where a lot of adults with learning disabilities start. What we desperately need is information about our condition.

One of the first things I learned was that I was part of 10% of the population that has learning disabilities. I had real difficulty in understanding how I could possibly have been walking around with 10% of the population that had the same kind of troubles that I had, and not known that they existed. It was a big relief to discover that I wasn't dumb, that there was nothing wrong with me; it was simply that I have language difficulties. This little bit of information seems quite simple and easy, but it has taken me years to really understand it. For those I work with, it's also the same slow process.

Techniques: Support Groups

I have learned a lot of very important things about learning disabilities in support groups. The people talking there are the real experts on learning disabilities, because they've lived with them. I have watched people learn about their disabilities and learn to compensate and follow careers or interests that they thought were impossible for them. I have run literally hundreds of support group meetings, or I should say I have facilitated hundreds of support group meetings, and I want to share some of the things that I have found that have worked for me. I hope that others will be able to do similar kinds of things.

I find meetings work best if they are not too large. Eight or ten people, or maybe a few more, seem to work the best. However, I have done these meetings with 30 or 40 people in them. We haven't been able to have everybody participate, but they have worked. I always work these groups in a circle, so that everybody is equal and everybody can see all of the others. I just sit in one of the seats in the circle, like everybody else does.

I find that the people coming to these meetings are often scared, sometimes angry, usually confused, and that it's usually a very difficult thing for them to do. One member told me that he drove to the meeting several times and only could get as far as the parking lot. After enough repetitions, he finally got up his courage enough to come in. Once he joined us, he became a very active member of the group and ended up being a leader.

The first thing that I always do is establish confidentiality. I do a little talk explaining that the things that we say here and the things that we talk about are okay to take with us, and we can even talk about them, but the thing we can't do is talk about people's names, where they're from or what school they go to, because it's so much easier for the folks to start telling their stories and opening up if they know that what they say isn't going to be part of the community gossip afterwards. I find that everybody is faithful to this, and it is a relief for people to know that they can participate openly.

If this is a new group, for the first step I go around the circle and have everybody say what their first name is and where they're from. Sometimes, depending on what the circumstances are, I might ask them to say the last grade that they attended in school. I usually lead off with my own information so that other people will know what's expected. This gives everybody a chance to at least speak, and you begin to get acquainted with people. Another thing that we sometimes do is all wear name tags with our first names on them so that people can start getting more acquainted.

I then take a little time to tell part of my own story about living with learning disabilities and a lot of the troubles they have caused me. I talk about going to school and failing over and over again, and being teased by the other kids or made fun of, and the difficulties that I had learning in general, and also some of the social problems that I had. I don't want to take up too much time with this, because I don't really need to tell my story; I have done it hundreds of times. But the others need to know what their story is, and they need to start telling it. They will have to work at this, sometimes for a long time, before they can recognize what has happened to them and get it into words to express it.

People may start reacting best to a direct question, so when I want to open it up, I will ask, "Did you have problems in school?" or "What was school like?" and see if people can start responding. Usually they can. And usually somebody will volunteer to start sharing some of their school experiences. After a little while, somebody else will have something to say, and you can get them to expand on what their experiences were. They might be a little bit different, but usually tough. After a while, everybody begins to see that they're not the only ones who had these struggles in school, or who had these struggles socially, and it's surprising how quickly people will start opening up. Before you know it, you've got some real lively discussion going.

If, for some reason, you don't get volunteers who want to start talking, you can go right around the circle and have everybody just say something about how school was for them. Another thing that can help is to have a co-facilitator. Martha and I worked together on many sessions. When we sat down in the circle, we'd be careful that we didn't sit side by side. When you start asking questions, sometimes the co-facilitator can start the discussion off by sharing a little bit of what their history might have been in relation to that question.

I've never facilitated a session that didn't teach me something new about learning disabilities for myself. The idea is to provide a safe, understanding environment so that people will be able to start sharing and discussing — open discussion. We need to understand, first, that other people have had the same kinds of troubles that we have, and that we're no different than a lot of other people.

As a facilitator, I watch to make sure that every single person in the circle participates. I think it is very important that everybody participate in one way or another. They don't have to have a lot to say, but if somebody hasn't spoken during the discussion period, I always call on them with a specific question that they can have a simple answer for, so that they will have participated in the group discussion.

I always take a few minutes to explain to the group that learning disabilities are not always in the same area, and that mine happen to come in language, but many people have troubles in advanced mathematics, and some people in both. We try to stay very inclusive. And I also explain to the group that it is their group, not mine. It is for them to discuss anything they want. They will have opportunities to lead discussion, they'll have all kinds of opportunity to bring in questions, or they may just want to discuss some aspect of a learning disability that is really bothering them. I find a lot of real good questions and subjects come out of the group itself.

One thing I've learned is that if you keep bringing new people into a support group, you end up meeting their needs by letting them tell their stories. But then you can't keep the group moving forward, getting into more complicated, more subtle parts of learning disabilities. It is so important for people to learn their story and to be able to tell it. However, these stories are all similar, and those who have been in the group for a while don't need the repetition. I haven't done it myself, but I have heard that in some instances it works well to have someone work with new members to help them get started and under-stand their learning disability to the point where they can start participating in the more advanced group. We could even call that a beginners' group.

Usually these discussions can't be productive for more than an hour. It is hard work, and we're asking people to do things that they can't do easily or naturally, so people get tired very quickly. Before you know it, the first session is done. I usually invite people to stay afterward for refreshments, to give them a chance to continue discussing their problems less formally, and to do practical things like arranging car pools. This social time also offers an opportunity for people to start volunteering to contribute to the group — they can bring refreshments.

Most of the groups I've been involved with have met once a month. However, I think that, in the beginning, it would be helpful to meet every week for a while. It takes several sessions for the group to get working together and seeing how it's all going to happen and starting to ask questions. But they do quite quickly; it's amazing, sometimes, how quickly people under-stand how to do all of this work.

I don't try to overwhelm them with materials for handouts, but it is nice to start having some materials. You also need to check with the group, because there are probably some in the group who can't read enough to handle written material.

On my way in to meetings, I would always think up a question to present to the group, if the group didn't have something for discussion. Questions could be like,

What is your earliest recollection of problems in school?

Were your parents supportive when you had school problems?

Did your mother and father both have the same thinking about your difficulties?

Many times, it wasn't necessary, but I was always prepared. Facilitating the meetings seemed easy, because I didn't have to do any preparation work outside — just go to the meetings and conduct them, and we all learned together.

After a few meetings, when people started getting comfortable, and were working well, I'd drop a bomb on them. I'd arrive and say, "Tonight we're not going to talk about disabilities at all; what we're going to start talking about is abilities."

You would think that this would be an easy thing to do. However, I found that it was one of the hardest things to get a group to understand. We all had been told many times that we couldn't spell; or people made fun of us, or found fault; we had troubles reading or with math; and most of us had been told over and over again that we could do these things if we would just pay attention, or just try, or if we were just interested. So we have a real good understanding about our disabilities; but when it comes to our abilities, it's something that we haven't even thought about.

I use Dr. Howard Gardner's theory of multiple intelligences as a tool for us to look at both our disabilities and our abilities. I heard him speak at a conference, and I could see that this was just what we needed, those of us that had learning disabilities, to start getting the whole picture of what our abilities and disabilities are. I found that it worked, but it took some teaching

100

for people to understand the different areas that we might be good in and the areas that we might struggle with.

A couple of years ago, when I was presenting at a conference in Michigan, Dr. Gardner happened to be presenting there also. I had the opportunity to meet him and shared how I was using his theory of multiple intelligences in support group work. He was very interested and asked for details about how I was using it and what results I was getting.

Gardner says we have an intelligence in — he's up to eight different areas now. When I first started in, he said six, but he's added a couple more. And I think he's justified in doing it; I think he missed out on some areas in the beginning. His list is as follows:

- Linguistic. This is everything to do with oral and written language — the ability to speak, understand, write, spell and read.

- Mathematical-logical. This is the area that I'm talking about when I say advanced math. It also includes logic; they seem to go together. Many people with learning disabilities in language are very good at doing advanced math and understanding computers.

- Spatial ability. This is the ability to visualize something that you might want to build or something that you would draw. Artists are spatial, sculptors are spatial, anybody who wants to do crafts, engineers, architects — these folks all can do things in their heads and see them, analyze them, design them, change them. I know how it is because that's where I fit in; I think that's my strongest ability. A lot of the people I work with also fall into this category.

- Music. People with musical ability can hold music in their head, play instruments, or sing. A lot of the people fall into this category, and because I am not musical, I marvel at the things that they can do.

- Interpersonal abilities. That is the ability to work with other people, understand other people, know what they're thinking and what they need, and maybe even know ways to help them. The counselors I have worked with in substance abuse have fantastic interpersonal abilities. Teachers have good interpersonal abilities.

- Intra-personal abilities. That's the ability to understand yourself, keep your life on track, see that you get done the things you need to do to have a successful life. This is a place where many of us with learning disabilities also have a struggle. I think that falls into the category of what we call executive function abilities.

- Body kinesthetics. That means body motion, which is the area that athletes are in, dancers are in, as is anybody who makes body movement and has to be well coordinated and loves doing it.

- Nature, Gardner's latest area, means an ability to understand nature and take care of the earth and like to be outdoors; it covers things like hunting and fishing and forestry — outdoor kinds of things. This category makes a lot of sense to me because many of the people I've worked with who did not fit into other categories seem to fit into this one. I've lost track of the number of people that I've worked with who are landscapers.

Many of these people with these fantastic special abilities don't recognize that they have something that other people can only dream about. For people with learning disabilities, learning about and understanding their abilities is the first step in changing their lives. For years they have been stuck in a rut, angry at their school or their job or the people around them, blaming others for their unhappiness. They need to understand that they can take control of their lives, and that they can and must change *themselves*, not the people or the world around them.

In addition to the ongoing support groups, some of which ran for years, I have facilitated one-time support group meetings with people in substance abuse and similar programs. These were people who had already started the process of understanding themselves and talking about their problems. I could meet with them and present a new perspective that they had not considered before, and they could get right into it. In substance abuse programs, I was always bringing in new areas to be considered that everybody was interested in, and I always looked good. In these programs, I learned lots about how to do support work, and when I went back on the outside, I used all of these techniques and I looked good again. For me, it was a win-win situation. I found working in substance abuse recovery programs a wonderful experience. Everyone was interested and was trained to be dealing with our feelings, the pain that we had had from our past experiences. Everyone was supportive and interested and generous In helping others.

One night in a group I had an older man who very obviously had learning disabilities. He could talk about all the difficulties he'd had at school, and all the things that had gone wrong in his life, but he couldn't say that he was learning disabled. He could talk all around it, but he just couldn't say the words "I'm learning disabled." I decided that I wasn't going to help him say it, and he was going to have to do it on his own or it wasn't going to get done. It happened that at the end of our session we had to rearrange our room, put chairs back and fix tables and so forth. So he hadn't been able to share with the group that he was learning disabled, and he was helping put the chairs back, and we were all working at it. He was getting more and more red-faced, and I didn't think that he was going to be able to do it, but I waited and I waited. Just before I left the room, when he couldn't possibly have done it any later, he blurted out, "I'm learning disabled, too."

We spend many years covering up and hiding our difficulties, and we just have to be able to talk about them and admit to them before we can deal with them. This man turned a corner, and was now in a position where he could actually do something about his difficulties.

Another time, I got called back into the unit to go one on one with a couple of guys I had worked with before and knew about. When I got in there, the counselors had thought that I should talk with them individually, but I knew that their stories were very similar and I thought that it would work better if I took the two of them together, and that's the way that I did it. It happened that both of these men, middle-aged men, had had all kinds of social-emotional troubles. They both had been divorced and had all kinds of family troubles, and just didn't have success socially with anyone. The two of them worked very well together and their stories were very similar. They were able to see that they weren't alone in the difficulties that they had — this fellow right here was having the same kinds of troubles. So they were able to compare their stories, and they were able to get right into the nitty-gritty of how their relationships had failed, particularly their marital relationships. We were able to have discussions about lack of communication, and how people have to have good conversations about difficult things, and share feelings, and respect other people's feelings, and listen to each other. These are the things that relationships get built on, and they hadn't been able to do them.

They ended up understanding that they hadn't failed because they were bad, or didn't care, or weren't interested. It was simply that they lacked certain skills, and these were learnable, and that's what they were doing; they were discussing them, and seeing how language can be used, and the kinds of things that they needed to do to improve their communication abilities.

When the session was over, I was walking down the corridor and I met a counselor. The first thing he said was, "Boy, did you validate those two guys!" (In counseling terms, "validation" is the recognition that the difficulties, problems, and feelings you're having are not abnormal, that lots of other people have them and have dealt with them and changed their lives. In other words, you're not as hopeless as you think you are.)

I said, "What are you talking about? You haven't even talked with them yet."

He said, "Turn around and look at them."

When I did, those two guys were beaming from ear to ear. They were just so relieved and so pleased with what had happened that they had truly been validated. They had learned a lot about themselves, and it gave them some direction as to where they could go in the future, and it gave them hope. That was the beginning of their being able to change their lives and do things just a bit differently than they had in the past and be more successful. I think one of the things that we overlook lots of times is that all we sometimes need is just a little validation.

The other area that I did support group work on a one-time basis in was at the state LDA conferences every year. For six or seven years, I ran a group meeting for adolescents at our annual conference. Out of those meetings, some very interesting things happened.

These sessions were run as I normally run a group support session. Martha was my co-facilitator for most of these sessions. I opened them up the same as I usually do by establishing confidentiality. Most of these people were high school age, but sometimes a few were a little older. The sessions were run for people with learning disabilities only.

The things that these adolescents wanted to talk about were the social and emotional issues, not the academic issues. In one of the groups that we were working with, after a little while I could see that they wanted to talk about their friends, or their lack of friends. It was something that I knew would be very difficult, so I made sure that I had plenty of time left to deal with it. I then opened it up to discuss how we were doing with our friends and how that part of our lives was going. When they started to discuss this issue, the pain was so terrible that they started to cry, both boys and girls. The pain was so intense even the facilitators were crying.

One of the things I have learned in dealing with these things is that oftentimes there is severe emotional pain to be dealt with, and I find that it has affected me also. But I did find that even though the tears might be running, I could stay very functional and keep a meeting going and help work through the issues.

These kids were saying that they didn't have a single friend in the world, and they would give anything just to have one friend. Most of them were telling the same stories. They end up with no one to eat their lunch with, and nobody to talk to before or after school or during breaks, and it becomes very difficult. One thing that helped right away was for everybody to realize that the others had the same troubles. Our advice to them was to start confiding in somebody about these difficulties, either their parents, or a counselor at school, or somebody at their church — somebody for them to start sharing with. We also suggested that they get involved in some kinds of activities that their disability didn't hamper in as much as it did in school – for instance, some kind of a church group or a youth group. This was a very hard session, but we did manage to get a dialogue started.

In that group, I had one young woman (she was probably in her mid-20s) who talked about having a problem in not under-standing relationships. She wasn't able to tell when people were really interested in her or not, and she said that she kept getting used. She told us that she had been engaged five times, but those relationships were just so that somebody could use her, and they never led to marriage.

Another year, the group that we did was really large, 25 or 30 people in it. Of course, we arranged everybody into a circle, took up the whole room. We ran the same kind of program that we normally do – we would share some of our difficulties. This group wanted to deal more with the social-emotional issues again. It happened that there were three young ladies in this group, and they had gotten acquainted before we got ready to start and sat down in the circle together. They were verbal and ready to talk about their issues. Because there were three of them, I think they gave each other courage to go ahead. Through them, we were able to get some unusually meaningful discussion going with the whole group.

On the subject of friends and friendship, they explained that they had trouble talking to the other girls, because they couldn't really keep up with their language. Sometimes it would go fast, sometimes they would be talking about the boys, or clothes, and they just couldn't seem to be interested or keep up or get into those kinds of conversations. But they had discovered that it was easier for them to talk with boys. They ended up having friends who were boys, and they wanted us to understand that they weren't boyfriends, they were just friends. They played sports with them after school — they might play football or touch football, and they'd end up going home with grass stains all over their clothes. They ended up always being with boys. In fact, they said their parents were going crazy, because they kept bringing these 225-pound boys home and their parents kept suggesting that it would be nice if maybe they had some girl friends.

Another area people with learning disabilities have difficulty with is that we don't have a good sense of style. We don't know what's appropriate to wear, or how things go together, and oftentimes we get in trouble for that. We had quite a discussion about all of this, and many in the group told of instances where they had been made fun of because they didn't wear what the rest of the group wore, or something wasn't appropriate. One girl had relied on another person to tell her what would be good, and she wanted to wear something a little bit different, and went off to school. But the advice had been purposely misleading and the other students made fun of her and it ended up being a disaster. They were saying that's it's always safe to wear blue jeans and a navy sweatshirt, but sometimes they'd like to wear something different but didn't know how to do it. And the three young ladies in that group were all in blue jeans and navy sweatshirts. When you're a teen-ager, these are all very important issues.

One year, we changed the program for our conference and didn't put in an adolescent support group meeting, because we wanted to try something else. That year, some adolescents

107

showed up and expected to have a group session. So we did put one together, to satisfy that real need.

Techniques: remediation and accommodations

In addition to dealing with social and emotional needs, it is often useful, even for adults, to do something about our academic needs. We are just like the general population; we need to know how to read, write, spell, speak, and do math. And we can be taught those things, even as adults, or we can learn to make accommodations for our specific disabilities.

In language, the most important corrective method is called *remediation*. We have to be taken back to the very beginning of our language education and start over with a new or a different type of reading program than we have ever had before. We need explicit, direct teaching of language. We do not have strong natural abilities in language, so have to use other methods to learn.

To begin with, we have poor processing skills. We don't process language automatically; we hear it all right, but we struggle with getting the information from our ears into our minds, and also, we struggle to get the information from our minds out our mouths. We can learn the rules or systems of language, but we have to be taught them explicitly; there's no way we can know them without outside help. For reading and spelling, we have to be taught the sounds of all the letters, and also the sounds of groups of letters, all the little bits and pieces of sound that make up language. These things don't come automatically for us; we don't pick them up by just hearing the language.

We not only need to learn these things, but we also need to learn to use them at a fast rate, or to develop *automaticity* in them. Many of the things that we do, we do through processing. This is a word that you hear me use a lot. We have to stop and think about these things, and get the information up, and it's a slow, hard process. If these things aren't done quickly and automatically, we never build what is called, in the academic field, *fluency*. This automaticity is developed by going over and over and over these things until they become automatic. It's a slow repetitious process, but that's the only way it will work. For adults, this is best done one-on-one.

We also need *multisensory* approaches. This means that we say words, we listen to them, we see them, we write them, we use all of the senses possible to get to understand and use language easily. We need multisensory, phonetic-type programming that is repeated until we achieve automaticity or fluency. Most of the research has been done on children; the same techniques work for adults, but of course the materials have to be appropriate, and it is harder to teach adults. We learn language the easiest when we are very young.

This remediation does work. I remember one woman who enrolled in a Literacy Volunteers of America (LVA) program, where the tutors had been trained by some of our educational consultants. She was in her mid-50s and had lost her husband, and he was the one in the family who always paid the bills and took care of the money and did the planning. He did that because she couldn't even read the bills and understand how much money was owed, or do the checkbook. When her husband died, she was at a complete loss as to how to manage her life and succeed. So she went to a literacy program and had a tutor who was trained to do multisensory phonetic reading, and she learned to read and write; she also learned how to handle her checkbook. It really changed her life, gave her lots of courage, and pleased her immensely.

We had her for a speaker at a joint meeting of LVA and LDA one night; she was going to tell her story. I was acting as master of ceremonies that night. I had spent quite a lot of time with her, because I was afraid she was going to be nervous and have problems. She presented and did a wonderful job, and everybody was congratulating her. It happened that the tutor was also going to speak, and I hadn't really been paying attention to the tutor. I noticed before she started in that she was scared to death and shaking, and I wasn't sure whether she was going to be able to make it. She did well, and the whole program was a real success.

This lady was lucky, because she had a tutor trained in multisensory techniques. If students who enroll in a literacy program do not get appropriate teaching, they will experience the same failure that they have had many times before, and it could be the last time that they would attempt to learn to read.

The latest research out of the NIH (National Institutes of Health) validates a lot of the methods that we've been using for teaching in our field, and it also has given us new terminology and better direction for things to do in the future. It is generally understood that the research has been done mostly for children; however, I see that the same methods can be adapted for adults.

Besides remediation, there are things that we can do to help ourselves that we call *accommodations*. A good evaluation will indicate what some of these accommodations might be, and they would appear in the evaluation as recommendations.

If it isn't possible to have an evaluation, there are a lot of things that can be figured out to determine what accommodations would be helpful. For instance, when it comes to getting a story, would you understand it better if you read it, or if you had somebody read it to you? For lots of us, the answer is we would understand it and enjoy it and get more out of it if somebody read it aloud to us.

Talking Books is a free government service, and it is for anybody that is physically handicapped or dyslexic. It doesn't cost anything; the only thing that we have to do is get a signed application from our doctor that we should have this service — a very simple form to fill out and very easy to get. Each state has a library of books on tape, and they also have the special tape players in stock. When your application goes in, you will get a tape player and catalogs from which you can pick out any book you'd like to listen to, from thousands of them. They will send you two or three of those books at a time and keep you with an inventory. You have all the books that you want to listen to, and it will keep you going forever. With this service, I started reading with my ears. It was easier, it was faster, and my comprehension was much better.

In addition to the books on tape, there is another service which is called Recording for the Blind and Dyslexic, which provides textbooks on tape. A student who needs a textbook that has not been recorded can send in two copies and the service will record the text.

There are a few people whose audio perception is so poor that they don't like the tapes. We've had several instances where we've set somebody up with a tape recorder and got them the books, and after they've tried it a little bit, they just couldn't make it work, so they would box up the whole business and send it back. This is sometimes disappointing, but it does just point out that we're all different, and sometimes our needs are different. Now I often advise people to check their audio perception by getting a book on tape from their local library and seeing how it works, before they go to the state service.

The new electronic age has opened up all kinds of possibilities for us. One of the things that we have difficulty with is short-term memory, so a little personal recording device, where we can put things down verbally and retrieve them afterwards, can be a big help for scheduling and things that we're supposed to do. Many of us have all kinds of difficulty with what we call executive function types of things, and this can be a big help with that.

Some of us who have dysgraphia as one of our specific learning disabilities can learn to write on a computer. It is much easier to press a key than it is to tell your hand how to make the letter, so the processing is simpler; and the printed outcome is more legible, because sometimes the hand refuses to make the letter the way you want it to. All we have to do is be able to type a little bit, and with the word processing we can have spell-check and grammar-check. A lot of people that I have worked with have been able to express themselves with considerable fluency once they got started on the computer. As a matter of fact, many of them end up with computer skills as a real strength.

Another area that's becoming better all the time is word recognition software, where you can talk to the computer through a little microphone and it will print the words right on the screen. This does take some training for the computer; you have to read to it some and get some language into the computer, so that it has a baseline for your voice. Then you have to be taught how to start sentences and paragraphs, put in punctuation and finish up the text. This takes training, but it is helping some people write much more easily.

A lot of the compensatory strategies are very useful in helping get our education. When I was in college and attending lectures, I couldn't take notes, because when I started taking notes, the process of writing was so complicated and difficult for me that I couldn't pay attention at the same time to what the instructor was saying. So all I could do was sit there and listen to what the instructor had to say and retain all that I could. Now, some dysgraphic college students can bring their laptop computers to class and type notes. Others can bring tape recorders to tape everything the instructor says and re-listen to it later. The tapes provide an accurate review and make education so much easier, particularly for those with stronger audio perception.

Students with short-term memory problems have difficulty copying assignments or other material off the board. In this day of copying machines, the quick solution for this problem is for the instructor to duplicate and hand out the material.

Testing is difficult for many of us. We have to work hard to read the test, and maybe even have to read it several times to make sure we understand exactly what the questions are, and then have to be so careful with the answers that we don't make a mistake. Lots of processing of language is involved, and it's very time-consuming. Sometimes all we need to do is have extra time in taking a test, and we can write our answers down and be successful. For other people, a strategy is to have the questions read and give oral answers. Another way that laptop computers can be used is to actually write the answers to test questions. Instead of those terrible bluebooks that we used to have to write in for tests in college, all we have to do now is to pass the instructor a disk.

One program that is doing a good job of helping people with learning disabilities here in Maine and, as far as I know, elsewhere in the country, too, is the national Vocational Rehabilitation Program. Voc Rehab, as it's called, is a federally funded program run by each state. Its first goal is to keep everybody employed. Voc Rehab staff work especially with people who have lost their jobs, or are going to lose their jobs. They provide retraining and education to help them find new — if necessary different — employment. Working with people with learning disabilities, Voc Rehab counselors can help with evaluations; they can provide funding for specialized help in education, including individual tutoring; and they can even provide funds for special technological equipment, like computers or whatever other accommodation will be helpful.

All of these accommodations I've been talking about are due us if we're evaluated and documented as having a learning disability. We are entitled to full coverage under the Americans with Disabilities Act (ADA). We are legally entitled to any reasonable accommodation that will help us do the job that we are wanting to do or get the education that we are after. All of the things that I've been talking about are considered reasonable accommodations.

Several years ago, I worked with a young surgeon who specialized in stomach cancer surgery. He had a very good practice, and his career was going well. He had become certified during his initial education because a physician watched him operate, and the certification was done that way, as it was for all students in medical school then. After several years, he was up for recertification. The recertification was done by a written test. When it came to reading, this doctor had real difficulty in comprehension. His strategy was that he read the questions out loud, and by listening to the oral sound of the question, his comprehension was good enough so that he would know exactly what the question was and could answer it and be successful in taking the test. However, when he was taking his test and reading the questions out loud, the proctor at the test decided that he had been exchanging information with another doctor taking the test and disqualified him.

The surgeon appealed to the American Medical Association, and the AMA wouldn't give him any accommodations to take that test. He kept saying that if somebody would just look over his shoulder while he was operating, he would have absolutely no problem in becoming certified; or, he could have passed the written recertification test if he had been allowed a separate room by himself, where he could have verbalized the questions and not disturbed anybody else, and there wouldn't have been any question of exchanging information. He couldn't get either accommodation. It would have been different now; under the ADA, he certainly could have had the accommodation he needed to become recertified. I don't really know how it came out, because he left the hospital that he was at while I was working with him, and I never did hear if he got recertified or not.

My greatest compensatory strategy is a wife that understands my language difficulties and is willing to assist in areas that I struggle with, but at the same time lets me operate the best I can on my own. This is a difficult balance to develop and maintain, and it has taken me a long time to learn that it is best for me to ask for assistance where I need it.

Learning to live with disabilities

When I first started looking at my own issues, I was amazed that nobody around me really understood about learning disabilities, and I could see that somebody needed to start explaining them. Although it seemed impossible, I decided the somebody had to be me.

So I proceeded to learn how to do that. It started, I remember, with a first talk that didn't last more than ten minutes, though it seemed longer to me. I found no way to prepare for this talk. As I continued giving talks, I discovered that I couldn't use notes or written material to help me, because that made the situation even worse. If I tried to use an outline, I would have to go into a mode to read the outline and find out what it was I was supposed to be talking about, and then switch back to an oral mode. It just didn't work.

So what I did was, I started out by telling my own story about learning disabilities. As a way to keep it organized and not forget any parts, I started telling it in the order in which it happened. That way, I could keep track of what I had talked about. This became the pattern for me to do talks. After a while, I discovered that if somebody asked me a question while I was telling my own story, I could tag where I was in the story, answer the question and proceed from where I left off. It seemed to work okay, and the more I did it, the more questions, interruptions and variations I could handle as I was giving a talk.

I was always very quiet and had very little to say, so as I started doing talks on learning disabilities, people started asking me how I was doing it. I had to stop and think to figure out just what I was doing. The important thing was that when I was talking about learning disabilities, I had experienced them, so I understood them and knew what I was talking about. This went a long way towards helping me get that information expressed in language.

In general, one of the things that helps me a lot is when I know "all there is to know" about a particular subject. I can see that is the way I was able to talk about and sell boats. For many years, Janet and I went to boat shows and I talked about boats with customers. Sometimes for eight or ten hours during a day I would talk about boats steady. The thing that worked was, I understood my boats and I knew everything about them, because I had designed them and built them. I had taught myself all of the language involved with boats and boating, and that way I had the language more accessible. I didn't have to do as much processing to get it out of my mind as I would with a subject that I wasn't that familiar with. The more I talked, the easier it got. As I look back, I see that this experience helped me develop automaticity.

A lot of people think public speaking is a very difficult thing, and I did, too. But now that I have done it a lot, standing up in front of several hundred people and giving a talk on learning disabilities has become easy. I think the reason is that I have complete control over the language that I am going to be required to use. There aren't going to be any surprises, any unknown things that I'm going to have to deal with. To prepare, all I need to do is understand what it is that I need to talk about on that particular day. I also have to spend some time thinking about how I'm going to get started. I mean by that, I need to have something to say about the area, or the location, or the people I'm working with in that particular area, just get a good feel for the audience, and I can go right into my speech.

A couple years ago, I did a keynote address for an LDA state conference. When we got there, Janet got hold of a conference brochure and was studying it over. She started to laugh, and she said, "It looks to me as though you're almost the whole conference." And sure enough, I was to present for three and a half hours, and then there was going to be a panel, and I was on the panel, too. It was a two-day conference, and those putting on the conference told me that the people on Friday would be all professionals, and the next day, Saturday, it would be all parents and adults with learning disabilities, so that I would do the same thing both days.

Friday, I gave my general talk on my experience with learning disabilities and the ways that I had learned to compensate and develop language skills. Saturday morning, I was all ready to repeat the material for the new audience. I looked out at the crowd, and I thought they looked awfully familiar. So I asked those that hadn't heard me speak on Friday to raise their hands. Only one hand went up — so virtually everybody had listened to me all day Friday and they were there again to listen to me all day Saturday. I didn't panic. I started with a quick review of Friday's talk, both for the one newcomer and to remind myself what I had covered and not covered. I was able to pick out two or three areas that I hadn't touched on Friday to start Saturday's presentation with new material. Fortunately, this was a very interested group; they wanted to have all kinds of specific kinds of information, and they participated, and we had a lot of open discussion.

I was very thankful that this sort of thing hadn't happened to me earlier, when I first started talking on learning disabilities, and very pleased that I had developed enough automaticity that I could plan Saturday's talk at the same time as I reviewed Friday's. My experience shows that, with understanding of our disabilities and with practice, we can become as good at public speaking as anybody else.

I now can see that there are several different areas that have different requirements in oral language. One of the easy places for us to start out and practice our language and develop better language abilities is to talk with somebody one-on-one, and do this in a quiet place where there are not a lot of distractions.

Another challenge, especially for those of us who have attention problems, is carrying on a conversation in a place like a store, where other people are talking and moving around in the background. Other loud noises, such as traffic or construction noise and other completely unrelated sounds, can be distracting. The problem is that, when we have attention problems, we tend to pay attention to all of the noise and can't filter out the part of the noise that is not the conversation we're trying to deal with. The only solution I know is to deliberately, almost physically, focus on the conversation. Again, this is something that takes practice.

Yet another different area is the cocktail-party type or reception-type conversation, where you're supposed to mingle and get acquainted with people. I've discovered that most people like to talk, and if I just introduce myself and tell them where I'm from and who I'm with or whatever, it opens up all kinds of conversation.

One of the social skills that people with learning disabilities often find hard to master is casual conversation, over the telephone or in person. One technique I use is what I call pre-thinking, that is, thinking about what the other person might say in a telephone conversation, or planning some ways to start a conversation with a group of people. Before I plunge into an LDA meeting, for example, I like to sit quietly in my hotel room and think about who's likely to be there and what I can say to each of them — ask one about her family, another about his trip, another about a project I know he's involved with. I have worked enough on this issue so that now you can put me down in a reception in Washington, D.C., where I don't know a soul, and I can function quite easily. My methods may not work for everyone, or for anyone else, but the message is that everyone can develop something that will work.

There's one type of language that I have never been able to master, and that's when there's a group of people (particularly people who are very linguistic) visiting and talking, and language comes out fast and easy. Everybody is talking as a group, and they all can find places to put in some comment or ask a question or share an experience. For me to participate when language is flowing in several different directions among several people is impossible; it's impossible for me to get my thoughts together and participate. What happens is that, if I have something I want to say, before I get it processed and ready to deliver somebody else will be talking, or maybe the subject will change, and I just can't get in there fast enough to participate.

As an example of what happens, one night Janet and I picked up another couple we know very well and hadn't visited with in some time. Everybody was kind of excited and catching up on the news and all kinds of questions; conversation was flowing very fast. The other couple happen to be very linguistic, and my wife is very linguistic. As it progressed, I had things that I would have liked to have said, and questions that I wanted to ask, and it just didn't work — they were moving so fast, and everybody was a little bit excited, and I just couldn't get into the conversation.

After I struggled a little bit, I just sat back and listened to the conversation and figured out how it was all working. I could see that they didn't have any trouble, entering in, listening and sharing, and it was because their language was so much faster than mine. It takes me just a little bit of time to process language and get ready to speak. It isn't much time, only a fraction of a second, but it makes all the difference. So after I listened and figured out how this all worked, I said to them, "I want you all to just listen to me for a few minutes," and I shared this whole explanation with them. But I had to stop them before I could do it.

My oral language is getting better and easier all the time. I can remember back years ago, before I had any understanding about my own language, that it was difficult for me to talk, and I didn't like to. I always was very quiet and stayed in the background. My wife is very linguistic, and she liked to talk. It worked out as an advantage — I didn't have to do all the talking; and I let her do the talking when we met socially with people and in lots of other circumstances. So, in effect, I didn't get the practice that I needed. Janet says I allowed her to do the talking for me. I think I did even more than that; I think I encouraged her to do the talking for me.

A while ago, Janet said to me, "I think you need to listen more." I found it pretty hard to believe that she would ever say such a thing to me. She also now says, "You need to be careful what you pray for."

One of the areas I still struggle with as an adult is short-term memory. For instance, I can't hold a telephone number in my head long enough to dial it. I have never found a solution to that completely; but the thing that does help me is, I have discovered that if I subvocalize, or sometimes actually say the numbers that I'm trying to remember out loud, I can hold four numbers now long enough to dial them accurately. This is an example of using

119

a multisensory technique — by subvocalizing, I can hear the numbers as well as see them. When we started using telephone credit cards, I had a terrible time. I was slow, and I made mistakes in dialing in the numbers. If I was too slow, an operator would come on and ask, "Please enter your card number now," and sometimes I'd even get cut off before I got the whole thing in. Of course, it all has to be done very accurately or it doesn't work. With practice, and with subvocalizing, I have now done it enough so that I do make out okay and very seldom make a mistake.

It's interesting that I struggle with random numbers, but all the numbers involved with statistics on learning disabilities I have absolutely no trouble in remembering. In fact, I know more of the statistics than a lot of the people around me, and have no trouble bringing them up when I want them.

I can get numbers into long-term memory sometimes, and that will stick okay. But it takes a lot of repetition and it takes a lot of time. I had difficulty in learning my e-mail password, but through repetition, doing it over and over again, I finally got it in long-term memory and now I never have any trouble with it. It did happen that we changed servers a while ago. My password was very long and complicated, and I had the opportunity to put in a new password if I wanted to. But I decided that since I had the old password in long-term memory, I would keep it and not struggle with another password, even though it might have been simpler.

Short-term memory is a problem with words, as well as numbers, for me. One time I had a boat to deliver to a customer in Massachusetts. He sent me several handwritten pages of directions to his house, things like, "you go to such-and-such a town, there's a filling station" — and he described the filling station in detail — and it might be, "turn right at that filling station and go to another building" that he would describe, and "make another turn." It was all very detailed written language, with all the turns that I was going to have to make, and how far to go, and how many streets before I made another turn.

I just simply could not hold all of that material in my mind and follow his directions. So what I ended up having to do was, when I found the place in his directions where I was, I would get the next turn figured out. I would go and make that turn, and I would have to stop and go over the letter again and get the next turn figured out. I did that, one turn at a time, until I eventually ended up at his house — a long, hard process.

Now this is a place where I can use one of my natural skills. I am very spatial, and if I look at a map of where I want to go, I can retain all of that information and I have a picture of that map in my mind. If I have a map to use, I can sometimes look at it and put it in my pocket and drive right to where I want to go. The day I delivered that boat, if I had had a map there would have been no problem at all. The customer was apparently very linguistic, and he was using his natural ability. I am very spatial, and I was struggling with his method. If I had been giving him instructions, he probably would have struggled with my map.

Now when I want to go somewhere that's new or find a new address, I run myself a computer-printed map of that particular area. My computer does the map, and it even puts a star on the map if I have the address of where I'm going. This works very easily for me, and I never have to stop for instructions or have any help; I can drive right to a destination with no trouble at all.

I've already talked about the way I use a grocery list to solve one of my short-term memory problems. I use lists often, and always hope I remember to look at them in time. I have an engagement calendar and try to note down each appointment as soon as I make it. Modern technology gives us more resources; for example, Janet and I gave our grandson one of those tiny digital recorders, which he uses to make spoken reminders for himself.

Visual perception is another specific learning disability for me. This has all kinds of implications in learning to read and write, but for this section, I would like just to discuss other things that bother. I see things, but sometimes they just don't register. Nothing wrong with my eyes, it's just that the information that I see doesn't get received and understood by my mind. Here is a typical example: In my boat business, I had a shelf that I kept all kinds of materials on for building the boats. They were things like drills, screwdriver bits, countersinks, center drills — all kinds of parts that tended to be round and about the same length, made out of metal. I didn't sort them out or anything; as I was using them and got through with the parts, I would put them on this shelf. I discovered that I was going to that shelf to get some particular part I needed to use, and it wouldn't be there. I was sure it was there, but for some reason I must have mislaid it somewhere else in the shop. I would search the shop all over to find that particular part and I wouldn't find it anywhere. I'd go back and look at the shelf again, and there it would be, just as plain as could be. I had looked right at it before and hadn't seen it.

This happened when I was first learning about learning disabilities, and I could see that this problem was tied to the visual perception problems. I immediately started thinking that the thing for me to do was to get some little boxes and put them on the shelf, and sort out all the different tools — put all the drills in one place and put all the countersinks in another place. That would narrow down the field I would be looking at, and it should help me decide whether the particular one that I wanted was there. But I decided what I would do was to see if I could train myself to inspect that shelf more carefully and be able to discriminate what it was that I was looking for, and that's the way I went about it. I started training myself to take more time, and it didn't take long, just a minute or maybe even less than a minute, to inspect that shelf thoroughly to make sure the part wasn't there or to see if the part was there. It worked; I didn't end up spending lots of time looking in the wrong place for things. So that was my solution for that problem; once I understood exactly what was happening to me, I devised a way to compensate for the difficulty.

This problem is sometimes called a figure-ground problem. For years, my wife would tell me where something was, and when I would go to get it I wouldn't see it, and I would report that it was not there. She would go and look, and sure enough, it would be right there. One of the things I've had to learn is that she's more apt to be right than I am. But I have been able to develop a system for looking more carefully for things.

I feel very strongly that we need to find our own solutions for our difficulties. However, we can't begin to do that if we don't understand what the difficulties are. You can't fix something if you don't know what the problem is.

Sometimes part of the solution is to teach people advocacy, so that they can get the kinds of services that they are entitled to. It's also very important that we get documented, to make sure that we can get these services.

I have had success working with adults and young adults, and one of the things that has happened is that, because of this success, I have been given harder and harder cases. It has gotten to the point where I'm working with young adults who are having really serious troubles. Most of these kids have experienced extreme school failure and some have actually been kicked out of their schools. They also have had extreme difficulties in their families, and their families can't handle it any more, and some have been virtually thrown out of their own homes. Many also have difficulties with substance abuse or issues in corrections, so their lives have deteriorated to a very low, complicated level.

When I interview these young adults, my main objective is to get their view on their problems with school and with their families, because usually they have a pretty good understanding of what their difficulties are. Because I'm an outsider, but one who knows how it feels to have learning disabilities, they are apt to be open with me about their lives. They are confused and scared; they want to find solutions. Three quarters of the time I have all the evaluations that have ever been done on them, and that helps me in the background work.

I certainly am not always successful, but sometimes I can

help parents and service providers understand what is going on with these young people. Often they have a complete misunderstanding of what the difficulties are. For instance, the kinds of things that drive a parent up a wall are actions that seem to be very, very irresponsible – a young person doesn't do tasks at the right time, or on time, or sometimes forgets them completely; doesn't do homework in an orderly manner; doesn't keep his (or her) room picked up and take care of things. These all look like very irresponsible types of behavior; it looks as though the youngster could do better, if he wanted to, but he just doesn't want to cooperate and become a solid member of the family. What parents don't understand is that youngsters with learning disabilities can't figure out on their own how to do these things. They have to be trained to do them. When I explain to parents how learning disabilities cause these behaviors, they can get a different view of their child, and sometimes this has helped.

Another thing I find sometimes is that the evaluations have not been particularly thorough, or they might not have covered some of the areas that I think there might be problems in. Sometimes I recommend that further evaluations be done.

Another area to be considered is appropriate placement. Included among these young adults are those who can't seem to get their lives organized enough to become self-sufficient and live independently. They remain dependent on their families for financial support and many times for a place to live and somebody to keep their lives moving in an orderly manner. Many times we have parents who have struggled with their children for years to get services in school and help these children develop, and it doesn't seem to ever happen. They moved through the school years and into adulthood and they're still dependent on their parents, and their parents are still struggling. These issues are also very difficult to deal with. My personal concern is that I'm seeing more and more of these cases, and it seems that we're having more and more serious trouble as time goes on.

Advocacy

We all know how important advocacy is. We start teaching our children at a very young age about how to get the things they need and are entitled to, so that when they become older they will be able to self-advocate. When we are in school, the law that helps and protects those with learning disabilities is IDEA, Individuals with Disabilities Education Act. This applies until we graduate from high school or reach the age of 21.

High school students with learning disabilities are advised to get reevaluated as late as possible in their high school careers, because currently an evaluation is valid for only three years. Students without the written evaluation results showing that they have learning disabilities are not entitled to any special accommodations. And students who do have documented learning disabilities do not have to ask for accommodations when they start higher education — each student can choose whether to disclose learning disabilities or to try to go through college on the same terms as students without disabilities. Those who do disclose their learning disabilities, and it doesn't make any difference whether they're entering a vocational education program or a college or a junior college, are protected under ADA, the Americans with Disabilities Act, administered by the U. S. Department of Justice. Any student with a documented learning disability is entitled to ask instructors for reasonable accommodations, such as additional time on written tests or permission to tape-record class lectures and discussions. These days, most college faculty understand enough about learning disabilities so that they will not object. Often, in fact, the instructor will suggest or offer ways to make learning easier. If the instructor refuses ("It wouldn't be fair to the other students"), the student's avenue of appeal is usually to the office of academic support, or guidance, or student support, or to the civil rights officer — different schools use different titles. This office typically has a direct line to the president or provost, and the normal result is a change in the instructor's position.

Sometimes students graduate from high school and get into vocational school or college and then find out that they have learning disabilities. They can't keep up with the greater quantities of reading and writing required, or they can't do college math. These students are not entitled to accommodations until they have been evaluated and their learning disabilities have been documented. So, if they are to succeed in college or vocational school, they — or a professor, counselor, family member, or friend — will have to figure out that learning disabilities are involved and find out how to get needed services.

It happens that the United States government has become very interested in helping those with disabilities. The reason for this is that we are making a real effort to get people who are on welfare or receiving any federal assistance off this welfare and productively back in the work force. The reason that the government is particularly interested in learning disabilities is that studies have found that over half of the people who are receiving public assistance have learning disabilities. So, for any real welfare reform, the government has to see that we address the problems they have. The government is not only trying to get people off the welfare rolls, they're also trying to see that education is more successful and people don't end up on the welfare rolls, ever.

As we've said before, people with learning disabilities have special problems in getting and holding jobs. Under ADA, they are entitled to the accommodations already described. Sometimes, however, people and organizations — including welfare agencies, job placement services and other governmental bodies — do not offer accommodations. This is when people need to have advocacy skills. If they have been aware since childhood of their disabilities and their rights, they will be able to reach the people who can help them. In most cases, a governmental agency that denies you services has to tell you about the appeals process. Many agencies have counselors or other human resource people to help employees with personal and work-related problems.

On the job, as in higher education, one of the things that you have to decide is whether you want to make a disclosure about your learning disabilities. I am fully aware that there are circumstances where you couldn't make a disclosure, because it could cost you your job, even now. But there is another consideration: in larger companies that are operating appropriately, people can tell the human resource people about their disability in confidence, and it is not supposed to go anywhere else in the organization. The human resource people can help you decide if you do need accommodations, what they might be, and how to implement them. You might be able to perform successfully in this manner. The human resource people might also be able to advise you on ways to make a full disclosure that might be beneficial. It is permissible to take a job without making any disclosure to anyone, and then you can decide how you might like to proceed.

As with higher education, if you never knew that you had a learning disability, but you find that you cannot do some parts of your job, you can go to the human resource people to talk about your difficulties. They should be able to arrange for you to get tested and evaluated to find out if you do have learning disabilities.

One of the things that the Learning Disabilities Association of America and other organizations are trying hard to do is increase public awareness of learning disabilities. We hope that people with learning disabilities, or their friends, co-workers, supervisors or family, will recognize the problem and look for appropriate services.

Some people still go through their whole lives without knowing they have a learning disability. Janet and I have been interested in folk art, and we found an artist way back in the country, up in Aroostook County, whose work we really liked. He was retired from working as a carpenter, and was spending his free time painting. His work looked a little bit like Grandma Moses', but not so big and complicated. We would visit him about once a year, and he would have his paintings displayed in the living room — three rows of paintings, one above the other, all the way around the room. They were old country scenes, with wagons and horses and farmhouses and barns and cows, painted on hardboard and framed with used lumber (sometimes you could even see a nail hole) stained dark. He even provided a string on the back to hang the picture, all for $5 apiece. Janet and I loved the pictures; we always picked out eight or ten to take home, and gave them as gifts for many years.

After a while, we began to wonder if this man had learning disabilities. On one of our trips, Janet asked him if he learned to paint in school. He very quickly said, "I never learned nothing in school," and was obviously in pain and started telling us how bad school was and how dumb he was. His wife and daughter happened to be there, and they were trying to console him by saying things like he had built 45 homes in his career, and he wasn't dumb, he was very bright. But none of this seemed to help; he still was in pain. Janet and I wished we hadn't brought the subject up. This man was obviously very imaginative and talented, and he was proud of the fact that he had done almost 2,000 paintings, but he never got over what he saw as his failure in education.

On the other hand, people who know about their learning disabilities and how to work with or around them can have happy and successful lives. I've had the pleasure of knowing four such people. All of them have accepted the responsibility for finding their own solutions, something they couldn't have done without having complete knowledge about their disabilities. Each of them has given me permission to share with you his or her individual approach to living successfully with learning disabilities.

I've already mentioned my friend Dale Brown, one of the first people I talked with about my own learning disabilities. Later, Dale and I worked together on the national board of LDA. Dale remembers how hard it was for her to write when she was in elementary school. She writes:

128

It took me hours to do my homework, clutching the pencil, struggling to write each letter. This, however, turned me into a good writer, because everything was well thought out. Before the pencil went on the page, each word was chosen carefully. I didn't have the luxury of draft copies until after my eighth grade typing class.

Growing up with a learning disability taught me to work hard and focus on my goals. Some people consider that to be a bad quality, calling it "hyperfocus." But it's actually an advantage to temporarily block out every distraction and complete a job.

Dale has a full-time job with the federal government. Recently she wrote a book on employment and learning disabilities. She suspects that growing up with learning disabilities gave her the strength and determination to devote her evenings, weekends and vacations to this project.

Joan Esposito was 44 and had a son who was struggling in school when her learning disabilities, and her son's, were diagnosed. Joan grew up in Liverpool, England, where, like me, she experienced years of school failure. Moving to California and marrying a man who hobnobbed with movie stars, she used her intelligence and oral language skills to conceal her disabilities for many years, at the expense of her physical and mental health.

Once Joan's learning disabilities were diagnosed, she took college courses in language and math specially designed for students with disabilities. She writes of the anger and frustration she and her classmates felt as they wondered why they had had to waste so many years in grade school and high school, not taught then in the same effective way as they were now being taught as adults. Because of her and her classmates' experiences, Joan and her husband founded the nonprofit Dyslexia Awareness and Resource Center, headquartered in Santa Barbara, California. I met her when she did some special projects for LDA's Adult Issues Committee.

Pat Kissire worked with me in LDA; she was the first chair of the Adult Issues Committee, before I took over the job. Pat grew up in a small town, where all her teachers knew her family and bent over backwards to accommodate her learning disabilities. Without any formal special education plan, she was allowed to do projects, give oral reports, take her time on tests, and use other ways show what she had learned. But when she went to college, she failed all her subjects. A psychology professor helped her develop new accommodations, but she still failed to get a college degree on the first try.

Pat now has her doctorate and works with children and adults with learning disabilities. She writes that finding ways around her disabilities

> ...has become a way of life for me. I have learned to keep a calendar, wear a watch that is digital and buzzes when it is time for me to go somewhere, write myself notes, read ahead, ask for help, have someone proof-read everything I write, tell people I can't spell, and a hundred other little things that make it possible for me to function in life on a daily basis.

Even more important, she writes, is her fourth husband, whom she calls her "guardian angel who is always there to catch me when I fail, pushes me back out into the world when needed, and in general takes on those tasks he knows I still have difficulty in doing." Pat says having someone like that to support you is essential to living successfully with learning disabilities.

Glenn Young and I were on the LDA national board together and worked together on adult issues projects. Glenn was not diagnosed as having learning disabilities until he was 30. His career then was selling beer at sporting events. At age 37 he started college, where he earned his associate, bachelor's, and master's degrees in three and a half years. He now works for the federal government as a specialist in learning disabilities.

Glenn sees proper diagnosis as the key to living successfully with learning disabilities. An evaluation and diagnosis does two things, he writes. First, it tells you that you have a recognizable problem that other people have, too; you are not lazy or stupid, and you can take control of your life and deal with your problems. Glenn writes:

> The knowledge that I was in fact LD liberated me and allowed me to face many of the emotional issues which had developed over years of failure and years of knowing I was different and never knowing quite why. With diagnostics I could begin the fight to become a whole person rather than a fearful and incomplete individual.

Also, a diagnosis qualifies you for special education services and school and workplace accommodations that you need in order to function successfully with disabilities. Accommodations are especially critical to adults' success, Glenn says; he needs accommodations for his work. Accommodations are not a way to lower standards, but a way to success for people who are qualified to do a job, but cannot do it in the same way as everyone else.

These four stories demonstrate again the point I've been making through much of this book. All of us with learning disabilities have different specific problems and different needs, and all of us must find our own solutions. It's our responsibility to find the combination that works for us; we can't expect anyone else to do it.

Solutions, K – 12

Academic solutions

In the 1970s the federal government passed a law, 94-142, which dealt with children in school with disabilities. We now call it IDEA, Individuals with Disabilities Education Act. This law sets up a process to ensure that every child has a successful education. It starts with an evaluation for a student who doesn't seem to be making progress in school or is having difficulties. The evaluation is designed to determine if the student has learning disabilities, and if so, how severe they are. If they are indeed found to be severe, the parents, teachers, special education director, and other concerned personnel sit down together in a meeting of what we call a PET, a Pupil Evaluation Team, and put together an Individual Educational Plan, or IEP. (The terminology I am using is from the State of Maine regulations; other states use other language, but the concepts are the same.) The plan includes goals and a monitoring system to make sure that that student meets those goals.

Under IDEA, the special education law, all children are guaranteed "a free and appropriate education." To begin with, I believe that all children are entitled to a free and appropriate education. I don't think there is much controversy over whether their education should be free, because in the public school system it certainly is. My problem comes from the fact that many children are not getting an appropriate education; they are sitting in school and are failing, sometimes year after year, and sometimes never getting services. Children should get an

132

appropriate education from the minute they start school, not from the time that they get evaluated and qualify for IDEA and get assistance, sometimes many years late. Furthermore, even if schooling is interrupted – by treatment for substance abuse or by incarceration, for example – an appropriate education should follow them. Even with IDEA, many times our children aren't being served with an appropriate education.

Our minds are all different, so our educational requirements are all different. For those of us whose intelligence or skills are in areas other than language, we need to have explicit instruction in this language. I find that, for all people, those who have to learn something in the areas that they're gifted in or good at or like can learn implicitly. Those who need to learn something in the areas that they have weaknesses in or are at a low level need explicit education. With this simple matchup we can prevent most of the school failure that we're now experiencing.

Over the years, we have moved more and more toward educating everybody with implicit education. The results have gotten poorer and poorer. Now, with the newest research and experience, we are making changes towards being more explicit, and the results are exciting.

The implicit education that I had in school was called "sight reading." This didn't work for me. It was the only thing that was available, so I became a real severe school failure. My children and my grandchildren experienced "whole language," another type of implicit instruction. This didn't work for them, either, and they had lots of school problems.

When I was in school, and when my children were in school, there was no such thing as special education or a special education department. Now every school is required to have a special education department, if it wants to get federal funds. The special education director and staff – special education teachers and educational technicians (as they're called in Maine; they used to be called teacher aides) – conduct the whole process of educating students who have been evaluated and found to need special services, whether they have a learning disability, a physical disability, or some other problem that interferes with their learning in the same way other students learn. This process is quite complicated and does take a lot of time and effort. However, we have seen very good results when it is done properly. Parents oftentimes need training to be able to cope with the whole process and understand it, so that they can participate and make sure their child gets the necessary services. The law says that the parent will be an equal partici-pant in the process.

Many times, this process is very hard on the students, because they don't want to be different from the other kids, and they want their schooling to go along the same as it does for everybody else. They feel like they're different or there's something wrong with them.

For many years, we have been pulling children out of the regular classroom and putting them in what are called "resource rooms," full or part-time, for their special education services. In a resource room, a special education teacher will work with a group of children who have learning disabilities and other prob-lems, including mental retardation, physical disabilities, and behavioral problems. These rooms have been difficult, because all the kids refer to them as the dummy room and the students as the dummy class, and they don't want to have anything to do with it. But in a resource room, students with disabilities get individual attention by specialized teachers who are trained in techniques for overcoming or compensating for disabilities.

In recent years, our educational community is well along in incorporating "full inclusion" in our schools. Full inclusion means that all children are in the same classroom at all times. Special education students sometimes have a teacher or a technician work with them in the regular classroom; otherwise, the classroom teacher has to work with them as best she can. Those of us who have learning disabilities understand the importance of having everybody fully included, but we haven't solved all the problems that need to be considered in including children and still making sure that they get their education. We have to figure out what program is needed, and then we have to figure out how it can be delivered in the full inclusion setting. Many times it isn't really possible to do that; we have to present some of the programming in a pull-out situation.

I am seeing that many people are being fully included physically but not academically, and the inclusion is taking precedence and the academics are getting dropped. A student with a learning disability sits in a regular class — and fails. He no longer gets the individual service he needs from special education teachers, and regular classroom teachers lack the training and the time to help him. As much as we'd like to fully include all children, we can't do that at the expense of their education. **It is possible to "fully include" children and at the same time exclude them from an education, their peers, and their teacher.**

I think that we have to put education first. If we consider first what services are needed for a particular student, they sometimes can be provided in a regular classroom. However, if they can't be, we have to offer them in a pull-out setting, and we have to make sure that that setting doesn't end up being called the "dummy class" again.

Everyone has to buy in to make IDEA work. I know of one situation where parents really had to advocate for their child to get the kind of reading program that that child needed. They went through the PET process and had an IEP set up for the child to get an Orton-Gillingham type reading program. It happened that the school didn't have anybody who could teach that particular program, so they hired an educational consultant from an adjoining town to come in and work with that student. Much to everybody's surprise, she taught the child to read. In that particular instance, nobody was offended, and the school officials said, "How did you do this?" They became interested in different kinds of programs for children who were struggling, and put together a program for the whole school. That school now deals with all those children who have difficulties, starting in kindergarten, and has made a tremendous difference in that community.

Children go off to school to learn to read and write and do math. When this doesn't happen, they become failures; they know the importance of learning to read and write, and they think there's something wrong, or that they're dumb. We tend to use our success in school as a measure of our intelligence. When we fail, it only means that we're not good at the reading and writing. Children need to be told that their abilities are in different areas. They need to explore those areas and find out what it is that they have skills in. Many children who fail in school might be excellent in sports, or music, or spatial abilities. These areas need to be explored not only by the school, but also by the parents. It is through this development that children can survive without losing all of their self-esteem. If the strengths are understood, they can be used in developing the things that you have to learn in school. For instance, if somebody is good in music, you can have them talk about music, you can have them write about music, and it will be easier for them, because they know what they're talking about in that particular area and it takes less processing for them to get the language up and share it with others and communicate about their strengths. Some children could be very successful at science projects, or a science fair. Other children could do a wonderful job in building something, or doing art projects. These are all ways for children to display their abilities.

Sometimes kids are dropping out of school before they get to advanced mathematics or science, the areas that they might succeed in, without finding out that is indeed their strength. The school has to try all students in these areas, because it might be the area that will build their self-esteem and produce a living for them. They will never know it if they don't get to it. Teaching calculus in second grade probably isn't practical, so the necessary solution is to do everything possible to keep children with learning disabilities in school as long as possible. If neither early intervention nor special education classes can bring performance in, say, English up to acceptable levels, there are still accommodations that can be offered.

Some schools have a policy of barring students from extracurricular activities if they are not doing well academically. Students with learning disabilities should never be punished for failing their English course by being thrown off the sports team or otherwise excluded from activities in which they do experience success.

When all else fails, social promotion may be the answer. In Maine in recent years, enough students have graduated from high school unable to read that the idea has become controversial. But it got me into college and a successful career.

We still have a lot of children who aren't identified and aren't served. One of the things that has been happening to us here at the state level is, every year as seniors approach graduation, people become aware of the fact that we have a senior in high school who can't read, and has never been identified, never been dealt with. All of a sudden there is a real problem. I've been telling my wife that they call in here wanting a solution, but it isn't possible at the end of the senior year to do anything for a child. To me, it seems as though they called the right place, but they did it 10 years late.

The schools have had to learn about learning disabilities and how it impacts their students and what their needs are. This has been a slow process. However, some schools have addressed these issues and have made some significant changes. I have tried to work with as many schools in my state as I can. I have done many in-service trainings for teachers in grade schools, high schools and vocational schools. I try to explain to them what it's like to be a student and not be able to succeed with the program, and how it feels to be an outsider and not really participate in the educational process, and also offer some solutions and what the kinds of things are that will work and will help. Generally speaking, these teachers have all been very receptive and very interested in my message.

Many times, I've also talked to the students. It depends on

what their needs are — sometimes it's just general information, and sometimes there gets to be friction between students who are receiving special education and those in regular or general education, particularly in the high school or junior high school years. When I explain that a lot of people — of all ages — have learning disabilities, the special education students immediately feel less alone. And often the students who don't have learning disabilities will be more sympathetic and understanding when they're given information that dispels the myth that learning disabilities are synonymous with dumb. Many top students can have language difficulties or math difficulties and be leaders in their class.

The long-term solution is early identification and early intervention, so that these students learn to read, write, and do math starting in the kindergarten years, right along with their peers, and never have to be remediated.

Early Identification

I originally started working with adults, and it was very obvious that their difficulties were stemming from things that happened way back in school. So I started becoming interested in working with school-age children and understanding about IDEA and how it works, what the services are and what the services need to be, how some of the instruction methods we were using in the schools simply weren't working for those of us that have learning disabilities. I could see that this wasn't going on early enough, that we needed to work with children and give them appropriate kinds of training way back in the first grade. As I worked with those children and with some of the teachers and educational consultants, it was obvious that the first grade wasn't early enough, that it needed to go back into kindergarten. As I started working in the kindergarten area, there were people that were saying it should even go back into preschool.

We aren't working with our students anywhere near as early as we should. It has to be done earlier, and it can be done more easily, and more effectively, and it can be done with larger groups of children. They can be taught to read and write if it's done properly, and these children never have to experience school failure. They can learn to read and write at the same time as other kids do, and they will have their reading abilities down early, so that when they get into higher grades they will be able to read their history books or social studies books and get their education at the same time as their non-learning-disabled peers.

This type of thinking is very compatible with the findings that NIH has had in their studies over the last decade. We are beginning to screen students as they enter school and determine which ones are at risk for reading failure. We are beginning to have some screening tools that are quite accurate. Some of the schools that I have been working with are screening during the first half of the kindergarten year and are ready to start giving appropriate services by the middle of the kindergarten year. Lately, I am seeing indications that we may have screening devices that will work with preschoolers, and this would be wonderful, because it would start the children even earlier.

It's interesting to note that more than 10% of the children are being identified as at risk for reading failure. You would expect that it would be 10%, those who have learning disabilities. However, we're finding that there are other children who need assistance. It appears to me that there are factors other than learning disabilities that have to be considered. For instance, one of the communities where we worked happened to be a bilingual, low-income community. In that particular community, the percentage of children who were identified as at risk was as high as 36%, because those children who hadn't had good language experience were getting identified as needing some extra help. In this school, they gave all of those children a multisensory, phonetic type reading program, paying attention to phonemic awareness, automaticity, and fluency. They found that those children came along very quickly, and that some of them even were able to be switched over to the whole language programs and succeeded with them.

I sat in on several classes in that school system and watched teachers who had been specially trained to do multisensory phonetic reading programs. It was amazing to watch these children who would normally fail in school learning to read and write and working with the language and being successful at it. It also was amazing to me to see children who had difficulties in language being supported by the teacher, and also being supported by their classmates.

In this school system, I was counting students in each class that I visited and some of the classes had as many as 15 or 16 children in them. They were all learning and being successful. They were being taught better and more easily than older children would be taught, and they were being taught large numbers at a time instead of one-on-one, as you would see happening with children who might be in the fourth, fifth, or sixth grade, or higher. This really confirms what NIH has been telling us, that language can be taught better and faster, the earlier we do it. We now have people who are working with preschool children, and I think this is very exciting.

One night after a service club meeting in Maine, a man was telling me that he grew up in a French-speaking home. When he went off to school, he didn't have any trouble learning English, but he had problems thinking in English. What he was doing was translating English into French, doing his thinking and processing, and then returning to English to give his answers. This was particularly difficult for him when he was taking a test. He used a lot of extra time in changing these languages all around to come up with the right answer and then writing the answer back in English. He said that it was so slow that he couldn't answer all the questions in the test. As a matter of fact, he couldn't answer enough of the questions to get a passing grade. However, those answers that he did have were all correct. So he started his school career being a failure.

For a compensatory strategy, he needed to have extra time

to complete a test, and he would have been very successful. On top of that, he also needed to have specific, direct instruction in language to help him develop his automaticity in thinking in English. This could have been accomplished through using the same kinds of instructional methods that those of us with learning disabilities require. In other words, techniques that are essential for children with learning disabilities also can help other children.

This man would have become much more fluent earlier if he had had this kind of instruction. He did report that later, he was able to do his thinking in English, and went on and was a success in school and ended up being a very successful businessman in his community.

A high percentage of people with language difficulties also have messy handwriting, called *dysgraphia.* I think the first thing we need to do for these children is not to criticize their handwriting, because most of them are trying their very best to do a good job and have a neat paper, which seems to be a requirement of most teachers. Some programs to help with handwriting are currently being developed. I think this is an area where we will see development in the near future. The thing that has helped many students is the computer. It is much easier to punch a key than it is to write a letter.

Currently, we are remediating children when they're older, sometimes even in high school. This remediation is harder at that time. Also, the students have missed out on being able to do all of the tasks that they should have done, such as reading or history or social studies. They are not only falling behind in reading and writing, they're also falling behind in everything else. When they get remediated, they may learn to read and write. However, they have missed out on great chunks of their education. So they are behind in many ways, and they never catch up.

I think we could do a lot more if we could get more adults with learning disabilities to speak up about their experiences and share, so that people would understand how prevalent it is and what it's really like. The schools have been using implicit type programs more and more over the last several decades, and those of us who have learning disabilities can't learn to read and write through these methods. We need to have very explicit type programs to learn. There must be changes in our thinking about educating students who have learning disabilities. This is difficult, because it requires very strong changes in the thinking of many educators. And the parents don't understand about this need, either, so they have to be educated. To make the changes that are necessary in a school setting, everyone needs to work together, the parents, the community and the schools.

For me, our best solution is early identification and early intervention. Children with language difficulties can learn to read and write if they get explicit, direct instruction in language as early as possible. We have to pay attention to things like phonemic awareness, phonics, automaticity, and fluency. Nothing should be left up to the students to learn on their own, as it would be in implicit education. These are some of the things that we have been doing in the LD field anyway, but now we are being very specific as to how all of these things should be done, and when, so that children will not experience school failure.

My experience is that this explicit instruction should be done by general education, starting as early as possible. Now that we have screening tools to find children who are at risk for reading failure during the first half of the kindergarten year (and perhaps earlier), schools can start giving appropriate services by the middle of the kindergarten year.

A lot of these children will not have difficulty in learning to read, and they will not need any special education services later. However, I don't want to imply that we don't need special education, because I believe we do. To begin with, millions of children in school have not had the benefit of early identification and early intervention, and will need to have a full evaluation and special education services so that they can learn the missed skills. This can best be served by special education programs.

Also, there will be some children who will still not function well, and when they get into the third or fourth or fifth grade will discover that they are having difficulty. These children will need to have a full evaluation and services as we now do it under special education, with the same protections.

For years we have tried to teach all of our children to read and write implicitly, and this movement has gotten stronger and stronger as the years have gone by. Those children that can learn implicitly have prospered. They have learned to read and write and have enjoyed it, and have gone on and have done well. Those who couldn't learn implicitly have failed. The process has been that those who have failed have been picked up later and identified as having learning disabilities and served under special education or IDEA. Many children have been remediated under this system. However, they have already experienced a great deal of school failure, *because the basis for services under IDEA is the achievement of failure.*

Advocacy

Parents need to be the advocates for children, particularly for young children who are just starting school. We have found that many times parents think that the school is the expert in what their children need for education and how their education should go. However, we have found that it is mothers and fathers who are the real experts on a child. They have had many years of experience with their children and know what their reaction to school is and how things are going for them. The parents have many insights that school personnel would not have. The parents have a lifelong commitment to their child. They need to understand that they have the best knowledge of what is right for their child.

Parents can become familiar with the latest research and help their child be placed in good programming from a very early age, to prevent as much failure as possible. If a child is older and needs special assistance in school that might be provided under IDEA, the parents also have to become familiar with this process and all of the rules and regulations involved. All the states publish their own regulations for IDEA, which are available to all parents somewhere in the state system, usually at no cost. Also, every state funds some kind of advocacy support network that has information on advocacy. (In Maine, the Maine Advocacy Service and the Maine Parent Federation, both based in Augusta, are the support groups for parents of children with disabilities.) The school operates under the state regulations, and it is very important that parents understand those regulations, so that they can converse with the school and operate with the school under the same system. We find that, when this happens, school people automatically have a lot more respect for the parents and are more willing and able to cooperate.

Parents can insist on an evaluation. There are very specific steps that you have to go through to get this done, and this is learned through studying the regulations. Evaluations check all of the suspected areas of difficulty, and even give subtests in those particular areas. As part of the evaluation, the evaluator will make recommendations for the child. Through this process, the parents and the school will start the IDEA process and hopefully find solutions for the student. If the evaluation doesn't seem to describe the child and doesn't look like the child the parent knows, there is also a process for having an independent outside evaluation at no cost to the parent.

This whole process looks pretty complicated and overwhelming to anybody who first starts. One of the things we in LDA of Maine found that helps a lot was to have training sessions to help people become familiar with the whole process. Also, we discovered that sometimes the advocacy efforts broke down because the service providers weren't familiar with the latest research and appropriate programs and effective types of remediation. We did trainings for everybody who was interested — teachers, counselors, administrators, parents, anybody who wanted to learn about learning disabilities and the latest research and effective programming. I think this was more effective in bringing about change than our efforts in advocacy.

Children can't advocate for themselves, so the parents must do this in the beginning. But I believe parents should bring the children into the process and explain what is going on and what is happening and why, as soon as the children can understand. This gives them more knowledge about what's happening to them. They need that explanation. They know there's something wrong, that things aren't working the way they should. It is much better for them to understand what's happening than to be wondering what it is and maybe even imagining that things are worse than they really are. **Some adults I have worked with are still angry with their parents because their parents knew that they had learning disabilities and never told them.**

There is nothing wrong with having learning disabilities. If we don't talk about it openly and deal with it aboveboard, that in itself says it's bad and we're not going to talk about it. Both the parents and the schools need to talk about this freely. I know of a sixth grader who went down to the school office and asked for a copy of his IEP. He said that he had a substitute teacher in there who didn't know that he could use a calculator. Junior high school and high school students need to be completely familiar with all of their IEP requirements, and they should also be attending their PET meetings. Many times, these students will have something to say that is very pertinent to their program. By the time students go off to college, they should be very used to advocating for themselves, because when they get away from home there will be nobody to speak for them; they'll have to do it themselves. And they should.

Nonacademic Solutions for Children

Children have executive function difficulties, the same as adults do, and these difficulties really need to be addressed and solved individually. I think the first step is to recognize them.

Children have problems remembering to get their homework done, taking care of their clothes, cleaning up their rooms. Their parents get upset with them over these things, and the children don't really understand that they have these kinds of problems, which haven't been described well and understood.

When I'm working with kids in school, one of the things that I ask them right up front is, "Does anybody have a mess in their locker, right now?" They'll start to laugh, because they know exactly what I'm talking about. When I was in school, we didn't have lockers, but we had desks, and my desk was always a terrible mess. Everything was thrown in there in a jumble; I couldn't find anything, and papers were lost. Now backpacks seem to be the culprit. I think our lockers and backpacks get to be symbols of our lives: terribly messed up.

The very first step toward a solution is to be able to say, "I have a problem. It's affecting my life, and I need to be able to get things straightened out and organized." This is a family issue. Everybody needs to stop and take a good hard look at what isn't working right, and have good open discussions on what the issues are. Then everybody has to brainstorm on solutions.

Executive function difficulties include not only disorganized belongings, but also poor time management, lack of social skills, and memory problems (short-term and long-term). The basic solution is the same for all of these problems. First, everyone — including the child — needs to recognize that the child has a problem and is not deliberately being uncooperative. Instead of assuming that the child is irresponsible and doesn't care, everyone needs to understand that the child wants to do things right, and needs to support him, not criticize him. Then the child, the rest of the family, and anyone else involved need to be engaged in thinking up ways to handle the problem.

People lacking time-management skills cannot organize their lives to get things done. Children don't know how long they've been out playing, when they're supposed to come home, when they need to start homework to finish it before bedtime. For some children, the solution is a watch, and in my experience, the best kind is a simple digital watch that gives you the time directly, with no processing (figuring out the hours and minutes) required. Many people I've worked with have become dependent on their watches, once they got used to them. For others, the watch is no help; they forget to look at it, or they don't make the connection between the time on the watch and the time supper is on the table. After enough mistakes, the child and the family will understand they need to come up with a better solution.

Outside school, as well as inside, children with learning disabilities need to develop their natural abilities. Parents see their children operate in lots of different areas – sports, building things, music – and their role is to support them in these various areas so that they have a chance to find the areas they enjoy the most and can be the most successful in. For instance, one of the families that I worked with called their son "the inventor." This was a strong clue to the area he excelled in. In every house where children live, but especially in houses where children with learning disabilities live, there should be a whole variety of things to experiment with and learn on, and a parent willing to supervise the use of them. In addition to books and videos, children need sports equipment, hunting and fishing equipment, tools for building, materials and equipment for handicrafts and art, musical instruments, pets to care for – and encouragement to try new things.

Also, children with similar strengths will be able to socialize much better together. This helps them develop their verbal abilities and find their place in the world. Children who just sit in school and fail end up also being social failures, and ultimately will not have any friends. This is a heartbreaking situation that can be avoided if we pay more attention and see that these children have opportunities in areas besides language and math.

Another point is that socialization can be taught in the family. For example, the parents can set aside some time every day, over a meal, for everybody to explain what they've been doing that day and what's happening and just general conversation from everybody in the family. Many of us with learning disabilities have difficulty with oral expression. The solution to this problem is to practice talking; but the natural inclination is to talk less, to avoid the effort. For this reason, parents need to encourage their children to speak up. Often, of course, one or both parents, and perhaps others in the family, will also have learning disabilities, so the deliberate practice in oral language benefits the whole family.

Sometimes parents have good intentions, but they don't understand the problem and therefore can't come up with useful solutions. For example, after one support group meeting at an annual LDA conference, a delightful young man was sharing with me his difficulties in verbal expression. He was having trouble speaking; as a matter of fact, it was so difficult he was even stuttering some. I started sharing with him about how those of us who have these expression problems are using so much cognitive power that we don't have anything left over to pay attention to other people. The particular difficulty he was having was looking anybody in the face when he was talking with them. I explained that this is just distraction enough so that you can't get the language ready and present it. He finally said that his father kept telling him that if he was a real man, he would look people right in the eye when he was talking with them. We had further discussion, until the young man understood exactly what was happening to him and what he needed to do to help himself. I finally told him that if he could tell his father exactly what was happening and how it affected him, I, at least, would know who the biggest man in that family was.

Another form of verbal expression problem is that of the child who talks too much without ever getting to the point. Language keeps coming out of them. They need to be taught how to get to the point and say what it is that they're trying to say. I've heard a mother say, "Tell me that in 25 words or less." The child needs to slow up enough to get the language thought out better before they speak.

All children need to have a good night's sleep every night. This applies especially to those with learning disabilities, since sleep disorders frequently accompany learning disabilities. One of our grandsons used to need white noise, like a fan running, to help him sleep better. In some cases, before resorting to special programs or to drugs, a child's school performance can be improved just by sending him off to school well rested. This rule applies all the way through high school; in fact, recent research has shown that high school students need as much sleep as younger children, or more, and that they benefit when classes are started later in the day, so that they can get an extra hour's sleep in the morning.

All of our problems multiply under stress, so we need to arrange our lives to reduce stress as much as possible. Being well rested is one way to reduce stress. For young children, parents have to assist in organizing their lives so that there is time for schoolwork and play without rushing from one thing to another. For example, a child with learning disabilities may need to get up earlier in the morning than the brothers or sisters, so he or she can get ready for school without pressure. As children get older, they have to assume more responsibility for their lives, which become more complicated as they need time to visit with friends, play sports, and do outside activities. Parents need to be very attentive and offer guidance, encouraging the children to do as much as they can, with the goal of the child gradually assuming more and more responsibilities.

The family is a safe place for children to learn and make mistakes. It's a place to experiment with language and try new things, knowing that when they make mistakes, they will not be made fun of or criticized; they are going to be supported.

I am constantly telling people that they need to understand their learning disabilities before they can do anything about helping themselves or making their lives better. This also holds true for children. Even though they are young, they can understand about their difficulties and their learning disabilities and start to deal with them.

The first thing they have to learn is that they're not the only ones with these kinds of problems, that there are lots of people – even lots of famous people – who have the same kinds of difficulties. You can also usually look in your own family and point out people who have had trouble with language and math, and they're no different than other members of the family. Teach children that there is nothing wrong with learning disabilities. It is okay; it's just that we're all different, and some of the things that we have to do, we have to do differently. For instance, they might have to do their school work differently than some of the other children they're going to school with.

Let's not spend all of our time looking at just the disabilities. Those of us who struggle with either language or math seem to get consumed with these difficulties. However, we have other areas that we excel in, and these need to be explored right along with the disability.

For instance, a lot of the kids I deal with have exceptional abilities in spatial projects. These are the kids who are always building things. One of the questions that I ask kids when I'm working with them is, "What kind of toys do you like to play with?" And oftentimes these kids will tell me things like, "Oh, I love my Lego set. I have the biggest set in the world. I can build anything I want with it." Sometimes they'll be teen-agers when they're telling me this, and they're kind of embarrassed to say, "I sometimes still get my Legos out and play with them."

Other kids I've worked with have real high abilities in music. They can practically pick up new instruments and play them right away, they retain music in their heads, they're always wanting to put together a band with other kids in the neighborhood. This is a real talent and should be supported and developed by the parents.

Many of these kids are excellent at crafts. They can draw, they can make things out of paper, or they can sew, or many other things. There are all kinds of opportunities for them to develop in these areas. Again, the parents can make sure that they have the chance to do this.

Other children are just naturally good at playing sports. This makes a good occupation for them, it gives them exercise, and it also gives them a place to succeed. This type of activity also needs to be supported.

Other kids have real natural abilities in working with animals. A lot of the children I've known have had horses, and that can be part of their lives. Others have got bug collections or snake collections. Dogs and other pets give children companionship and teach them responsibility. Some children are planting things; they love to have garden things growing. These are all good, positive things that can be developed quite easily.

When I'm training people about learning disabilities, I try to spend as much time on abilities as I do on disabilities. Often, children with language difficulties are unpopular because they communicate so awkwardly. Doing something they enjoy with others with the same interests and abilities helps them function much better, because they have so much in common with the others. It gives them a steppingstone toward building their language abilities and their social relationships.

One of the basic things that helps children with learning disabilities is to live in a structured household — specific times to play, to do homework, to do chores around the house, to eat, to get things ready to go to school, and to go to bed. These are things that take training, but they need to be done. In some households of children with learning disabilities, the parents also have some of these kinds of problems, so it will be a benefit to the whole household to get these things in practice. We can't just spend our lives watching television and expect all these things to become done. But we should be able to watch television sometimes.

People with learning disabilities, even children, shouldn't be excused from doing anything. Everyone can participate in family things like chores, keeping their rooms neat, doing their homework. The only thing that has to be figured out is *how* they're going to do it, because they may have to do it differently than you would expect. For example, a child might take a picture of his room all straightened up, with things in their places, so that he can check the picture to make sure things are where they should be. This could work with the basement or the garage, too, if it's his chore to clean them up and arrange them. Or a picture will show what the setup of the dining room table should be. I have talked before about the family having to brainstorm to figure out how these things could be done.

Many of us with learning disabilities also have short-term memory problems. We have the best intentions of doing something, and somehow it drops right out of our mind and gets lost forever. As another part of that, lots of times we forget how to do things. We become great procrastinators. We hate to get going on a project because it is difficult for us to do. We sometimes don't have any idea how to do it, and we start playing the game, "Well, let's put it off." I think that one of the things we need is to have strategies so that we do know how to do these things, and then it isn't so hard for us to get started.

To deal with the problem of our being able to find things, we have to keep organized. Everything has a place, and everything is kept in its place. This is difficult to start with, but as we get used to doing it, the rewards are high, and it makes life easier. I think we can see that it is something that needs to be done, and we will do it.

To accomplish this, things (such as our rooms) need to be picked up — they need to be organized. Our homework needs to be organized. This is all part of being in a structured family.

One of the things people have trouble with is selecting the clothing that they're going to wear. This interferes with getting your things ready to go to school the next day. If you have somebody who will work with you, you can put on several sets of your clothes and have your picture taken in each, so that you can see what goes with what and go off to school with some confidence that the things you have on match. From the pictures, you might discuss with an adult or a brother or sister who has some sense of style what might work for mixing the clothes from the different pictures.

152

If you can't read, get an adult to read you things that you would like to know about — for instance, directions for doing things, or notes. Anything that you're curious about and you want to know, make sure that somebody reads it for you.

Be wild,

be innovative,

and also

be successful!

Conclusion

To have learning disabilities doesn't mean to be dumb. In fact, it's quite the contrary. People with learning disabilities, by definition, have at least average intelligence, and run all the way up through very superior. Albert Einstein, whose brilliant theories about the nature of the universe revolutionized science in his time, had all kinds of language and organizational problems and couldn't do simple arithmetic. Winston Churchill, who not only led Great Britain through World War II, but also found time to write multivolume histories that are still respected, had all kinds of trouble in elementary school.

"Learning disability" only means that we don't have natural abilities in oral language, written language, simple arithmetic, and/or math. (See Appendix A for more details.) In contemporary America, language and math are the keys to communication and to school success.

We as a nation have tried to educate all of our children in language and math implicitly. It simply hasn't worked. Those who haven't been able to learn in this way have sat in classrooms and failed. Lack of a successful education leads to failure in all aspects of our lives, such as social interaction, emotional stability, health, success in our jobs, and success in relationships. All these failures lead to low self-esteem, depression, and behavioral problems. Even people like me, who can have a career and support a family, still pay a heavy price.

Research shows that the incidence of learning disabilities in the general population is 10%. It also shows that among people with substance abuse problems, in the correctional system, unemployed, on welfare or homeless, the incidence is at least 50%, and in some areas it is much higher.

In the last decade, a lot of research has been done on children learning to read. The results are very, very positive. The research is showing that those with learning disabilities need to have explicit, direct instruction. To meet these needs, we now have screening tools that will identify the children who are at risk for reading failure. This allows children to have a reading program that they will be successful with way back in the kindergarten year. They get their education right along with the rest of the children, so they don't ever experience school failure.

Up to this point, most of the research has been concentrated in the area of reading. But there is more to being learning-disabled than having difficulty in reading. Another thing we need to know more about and have more research in is math disability. Poor memory, organizational skills, and emotional aspects of learning disabilities need to be looked at now, too, and some research is starting in those areas. We also need to know a lot more about helping solve problems for the adults.

Adults with learning disabilities can make changes in their lives. First they have to understand exactly what their disability is, and they also have to know and understand what their abilities are. Many times we have been so involved with our disability that we haven't had the opportunity and time to learn about our abilities. Between the two, many solutions can be found. Adults can be remediated; they can use some of the same techniques that we have learned to use with children. It isn't as easy as it would have been when they were in the first grade, but it can be done. It takes longer, and needs to be done one-on-one.

It is also helpful for adults to have counseling to understand what has happened to them through relationships, their education, and their job experiences, so that their difficulties won't be repeated. Most adults also need training in how to advocate for themselves. They have many rights, but most of these people have not been able to benefit from those rights because they don't know what they are or how to access them.

This is a very exciting time to be involved in the learning disabilities field. We know so much more now about how to approach these problems, and we're beginning to see some real success. Now the challenge is to redirect some of our resources to help people with learning disabilities find ways to work around their disabilities and work with their abilities. It's an investment that will ease tensions and failures in school, take some of the burden off our law enforcement and correctional systems, and pay off in lots of other valuable ways. Best of all, it will restore a proper sense of dignity and self-worth to the 10% of us whose only "problem" is that we learn in different ways than other people do. When each of us can make full use of our abilities, everyone will be better off.

Appendix

Definitions

I. "Learning Disability" and Subtypes of Learning Disabilities

In 1990, the National Joint Committee on Learning Disabilities agreed on the following definition of the term:

> *Learning disabilities* is a generic term that refers to a heterogeneous group of disorders manifested by significant difficulties in the acquisition and use of listening, speaking, reading, writing, reasoning, or mathematical abilities. These disorders are intrinsic to the individual, presumed to be due to central nervous system dysfunction, and may occur across the life span. Problems in self-regulatory behaviors, social perception, and social interaction may exist with learning disabilities, but do not by themselves constitute a learning disability....

On its web page on learning disabilities,

www.nimh.nih.gov/publicat/learndis.htm

the National Institute of Mental Health (NIMH) describes a learning disability as

> "a disorder that affects people's ability to either interpret what they see and hear or to link information from different parts of the brain."

Disabilities are recognized by such symptoms as "specific difficulties with spoken and written language, coordination, self-control or attention." Frequently, but not always, people

157

will have more than one learning disability. A reference book called the Diagnostic and Statistical Manual of Mental Disorders, or DSM, describes ways to diagnose different kinds of learning disabilities, and to differentiate between delay in learning and a learning disability.

For many years we have been saying that learning disabilities are hidden disabilities, or invisible, because they can't be seen. However, in recent studies with MRIs (Magnetic Resonance Imaging), learning disabilities can be seen for the first time. Scientists see differences in the brains of people with learning disabilities compared to the brains of people without such disabilities.

According to NIMH, there are three categories of learning disabilities: "developmental speech and language disorders," "academic skills disorders," and other disorders. Within each category are specific disorders.

Among common speech and language disorders, NIMH lists problems with articulation, expression, and reception. A child with an articulation disorder may not speak at a normal rate or may not pronounce certain sounds correctly, and may not outgrow these traits as soon as he or she should. A child with an expressive language disorder cannot find the words or the sentence structures to speak appropriately for his or her age. A child (or adult) with a receptive language disorder does not make appropriate connections between language spoken by other people and the response he or she should make. NIMH describes the situation as:

> It's as if their brains are set to a different frequency
> and the reception is poor....Their hearing is fine, but
> they can't make sense of certain sounds, words, or sen-
> tences they hear. They may even seem inattentive.

Academic skills disorders include reading, writing, and arithmetic disorders, according to NIMH. The technical names for these disorders are *dyslexia* (difficulty in processing language, which interferes with reading as well as writing and spelling), *dysgraphia* (difficulty either in the motor skills of writing or in connecting the word visualized in the mind to the word printed on paper), and *dyscalculia* (difficulty with math skills and computation). NIMH points out that all three of these basic educational skills require complex simultaneous actions, both physical — moving the eyes or hand or both — and mental — paying attention, recognizing symbols and comparing present symbols to memorized symbols and ideas. Any "miswiring" in the brain that disrupts any one of the several processes can make it difficult for a student to read, write, or calculate, and may require special training to work around the problem.

Other learning disabilities include "motor skills disorders" and other developmental disorders, including coordination and memory disorders.

Another definition comes from the National Center for Learning Disabilities (NCLD) web page (www.ncld.org/info.index.cfm). This group, a coordinator for organizations dealing with learning disabilities, defines learning disabilities as

> "neurological disorders that interfere with a person's ability to store, process, or produce information, and create a 'gap' between one's ability and performance."

NCLD lists three other specific problems, in addition to dyslexia, dysgraphia, and dyscalculia:

- Dyspraxia is "a difficulty with motor planning" which makes it hard for a person to "coordinate appropriate body movements."

- A lack of auditory discrimination means a person cannot register the differences between speech sounds, or cannot understand how sounds are arranged into words.

- Problems with visual perception make it hard for a person to process what the eyes see, and therefore hard to make sense out of the visible environment, including written language.

NCLD points out that a learning disability is different from mental retardation (many people with learning disabilities have above-average intelligence), autism, a physical problem like deafness or blindness, or a behavioral disorder.

NIMH and NCLD list attention disorders — widely known in the popular press as ADD (Attention Deficit Disorder) and ADHD (Attention Deficit Hyperactivity Disorder) — as a separate type of problems often associated with learning disabilities. People with ADD cannot focus their attention; they are easily distracted and disorganized. NIMH says that many people with ADD, especially boys, are also hyperactive:

> ...hyperactive children can't sit still. They blurt out answers and interrupt. In games, they can't wait their turn....Because of their constant motion and explosive energy, hyperactive children often get into trouble with parents, teachers, and peers.

Learning disabilities are not uncommon. Because some children's learning disabilities are still not recognized, and many adults do their best to hide their disabilities, it is hard to get firm figures. For years, the estimate that 10% of the population has some kind of learning disability has been widely circulated. NCLD quotes a U. S. Department of Education estimate that more than 17% of children in this country will have problems learning to read, and says that about 5% of public-school children get special education services because they have been identified as having one or more learning disabilities. This 5% amounts to more than 2,800,000 children, according to NCLD.

No one knows what causes a learning disability. NIMH and NCLD list several possible causes that scientists are investigating. Learning disabilities may be partly hereditary, since they tend to run in families. They may result from improper brain development before a child is born; and such improper development may be a random mutation or may be caused by some accident to or action by the pregnant mother. Or learning disabilities may develop as a result of factors affecting the very young child; the two web sites suggest that head injuries, environmental poisons like lead and cadmium, insufficient nutrition, abuse or cancer therapy could be contributing factors.

Because of the growing suspicion that environmental pollution affecting unborn and very young children is a cause of learning disabilities, in February 2000 the Assembly of Delegates of the Learning Disabilities Association of America approved a resolution calling for more prenatal research and more attention to potential effects of toxins, pollutants, and chemicals on fetuses and children. LDA advocates cooperation and information-sharing among educators, public health officials, and environmental organizations.

As I have pointed out, the time to begin helping children with learning disabilities is before they go through a series of school failures that undermines their self-confidence and damages their relationship with their classmates. However, detecting learning disabilities in a preschool child is not always easy, because children vary so widely in their development. Here are some things to watch out for:

- Many of these children appear to be clumsy. They can't catch or throw a ball. They have trouble hopping or standing on one foot. They can't walk on a straight line. They can't shut their eyes and touch their nose with one finger. They can't tap each finger to their thumb on the same hand.

- Many of these children have speech and/or language problems. They learn to talk much later than their brothers or sisters or other children of their age. They mispronounce words (like *basgetti* for *spaghetti*), and use incorrect forms for words (like "We comed to the store") long after other children of their age. They have trouble finding the words they want to use, so they often use *thing* or *that place* or *that time* even when they've known the right words for a long time. They don't hear rhymes, so they don't enjoy some of the nursery rhymes or the books that depend on rhymes for meaning or for humor. In fact, I know from experience that we also have trouble mimicking things like accents, bird calls, and machinery sounds.

- Many of these children have a hard time remembering instructions or the sequence of things. They may go to their room to get a toy and then can't remember what they were going to get. They may be told that they are going to Grandma's house and then to the park, but when they get to Grandma's they're confused because they thought they were going to the park first. They may have a much harder time learning to say the alphabet or the counting numbers than other children of their age.

There is current research on designing a preschool screening test. The most important time for the school to evaluate a child is during the first few months of kindergarten. All children should be given a test of phonemic awareness and a test of how fast they can name colored dots or objects. This is called Rapid Automatic Naming (RAN). It will take teachers only about five minutes per child to give these two tests, and the children who do poorly on them are most likely to be the ones who will have trouble learning to read. They will need very explicit instruction on taking words apart into their separate sounds and putting the sounds back together to make words. They will also need explicit instruction on how the sounds of our language match the letter patterns we use for them.

Many of the characteristics that I described for preschool children can also be seen in older children. In her book, *The Learning-Disabled Child: Ways That Parents Can Help* (John F. Blair, Publisher, 1980; seventh printing, 1991), Suzanne H. Stevens lists some common indications that a child has a learning disability. In addition to the problems with reading and writing already mentioned, she suggests parents look for several of the following:

"Mixed Dominance" – where most people favor either their right (usually) or left hand, foot and eye, children with mixed dominance use both, or are right-handed but left-footed.

"Directional Confusion" – many people with learning disabilities can't remember which way is right and which way is left.

"Extreme Difficulty with Sequencing" – people with learning disabilities have trouble keeping items in order, and therefore are slow to learn the alphabet, the months of the year, the home telephone number and other such basics.

"Difficulty with Time or Time Relationships" – people with learning disabilities often are slow to learn to read a clock or watch; additionally, they often lack the internal clock that lets other people know how much time has passed.

"Poor Motor Control" – people with learning disabilities may have either large-muscle problems, which make them clumsy and poor at sports, or small-muscle problems, which interfere with writing, or both.

II. Educational Terms

Automaticity is the ability to handle language without using cognitive power, or in other words thinking power, to do it. This requires repetition and practice so that the language becomes automatic and you don't have to stop and process it all the time. Most of the things we do in our daily lives are automatic, like brushing our teeth, tying our shoes, riding a bicycle; we don't have to stop and think about each motion as we do it. We need to have automaticity in language so that we can read and write without tying our mind up in the processing. The mechanics need to be automatic, so that we can both understand information that we're getting and plan and organize information that we want to share.

Explicit education requires that the teacher give direct instruction until the student understands the material. This may require repetition, extra explanation and varied techniques until the student retains the material automatically.

A single person may require explicit education in one area, while implicit education may be very appropriate in another area. The message is that we do not all need the same type of instruction, and we may require one type of instruction in a particular area and another type of instruction in a different area.

Fluency is the condition that you're trying to achieve so that you can handle language without its being a cognitive process. It becomes quick and accurate. Because you develop automaticity in language, you become fluent in language.

Implicit education is the process by which we teach by providing good opportunity to learn, the materials to use, and a learning environment. The student is expected to explore, experience, and learn, and the teacher guides and evaluates the result. My first reading instruction was called *sight reading*. This was very implicit, and it simply did not work. In the last few years, we have been using *whole language*, which is very implicit, and has not worked for many students like me.

Multisensory is using more than one sense to understand language. For instance, if you see written language and hear it at the same time, between the two your comprehension and speed might increase considerably.

Phonemic awareness is the ability to hear all the little bits and pieces of the sound in language, so that you can understand how the different sounds in words can be represented by letters. Those of us who have difficulty in language usually have poor phonemic awareness. Phonemic awareness is something that can be taught.

Appendix

Some of the Principal Organizations in the United States that Deal with Learning Disabilities

As more and more people like me found out that learning disabilities are a recognizable phenomenon shared by a large number of people, organizations were formed to study and try to resolve our issues. The one I had most to do with is the Learning Disabilities Association of America (LDA). In the next few pages, I'll tell you a little about it and about some of the other organizations in the field.

The quoted descriptions come from the public information of these organizations. Most quotes come from their websites, where you can find out more about each one.

COORDINATED CAMPAIGN FOR LEARNING DISABILITIES (CCLD)

Telephone: 1-888-478-6463
Internet: www.aboutld.org

As its name suggests, CCLD, which is supported by the Emily Hall Tremaine Foundation, is a coordinating agency for six nonprofit organizations dealing with learning disabilities. CCLD helps the other organizations increase public awareness of learning disabilities and offer information and resources.

DIVISION FOR LEARNING DISABILITIES OF THE COUNCIL FOR EXCEPTIONAL CHILDREN (DLD)

Headquarters: CEC, 1110 North Glebe Road, Suite 300,
Arlington, VA 22201-5704
Telephone: 1-800-CEC-SPED (1-800-232-7733)
Internet: www.dldcec.org

The Council for Exceptional Children (CEC) is "the largest international professional organization dedicated to improving educational outcomes for individuals with exceptionalities, students with disabilities, and/or the gifted. CEC advocates for appropriate governmental policies, sets professional standards, provides continual professional development, advocates for newly and historically underserved individuals with exceptionalities, and helps professionals obtain conditions and resources necessary for effective professional practice."

The Division of Learning Disabilities of the Council for Exceptional Children (DLD/CEC) is an international professional organization. Its mission is "to improve the education and life success of individuals with learning disabilities." To achieve this goal, the DLD "advocates on behalf of individuals with learning disabilities; promotes best educational practices; provides forums for discussion of related issues; provides professional development for those concerned with the education of individuals with learning disabilities; recommends professional standards; encourages interdisciplinary interaction."

HELLO FRIEND / ENNIS WILLIAM COSBY FOUNDATION

Headquarters: PO Box 4061, Santa Monica, CA 90411
Internet: www.hellofriend.org

The Hello Friend / Ennis William Cosby Foundation is a nonprofit organization established in 1997 by Drs. William H. and Camille O. Cosby, in memory of their son. It is "dedicated to being a friend to all people with dyslexia and language-based learning differences, recognizing and celebrating their gifts, opening the doors of learning to them, and helping them reach their full potential." The foundation "promotes early recognition, compassionate understanding, and effective education."

INTERNATIONAL DYSLEXIA ASSOCIATION (IDA)

Headquarters: 8600 LaSalle Road,
Chester Building, Suite 382,
Baltimore, MD 21286-2044
Telephone: messages, 1-800-ABCD123
(1-800-222-3123); 410-296-0232
Internet: www.interdys.org

The International Dyslexia Association (formerly the Orton Dyslexia Society, named for Dr. Samuel T. Orton) is an international nonprofit "scientific and educational organization dedicated to the study and treatment of dyslexia." IDA works "nationally and locally on issues such as legislation, public awareness, research, public information and education," and collaborates with other learning disabilities organizations. IDA's mission statement says:

> "We believe that all individuals have the right to achieve their potential, that individual learning abilities can be strengthened and that social, educational and cultural barriers to language acquisition must be removed.
>
> The International Dyslexia Association actively promotes effective teaching approaches and related clinical educational intervention strategies for dyslexics. We support and encourage interdisciplinary study and research. We facilitate the exploration of the causes and early identification of dyslexia and are committed to the responsible and wide dissemination of research-based knowledge."

LEARNING DISABILITIES ASSOCIATION OF AMERICA (LDA)

Headquarters: 4156 Library Road, Pittsburgh, PA
Telephone: 412-341-1515; 888-300-6710
Internet: www.ldaamerica.org

LDA is a national, nonprofit, volunteer organization, including individuals with learning disabilities, their families, and professionals. LDA's purpose is "to advance the education and general welfare of children and adults of normal or potentially normal intelligence who manifest disabilities of a perceptual, conceptual, or coordinative nature" and to alleviate the restricting effects of these disabilities. LDA's mission statement says that the organization is

"dedicated to identifying causes and promoting prevention of learning disabilities and to enhancing the quality of life for all individuals with learning disabilities and their families by encouraging effective identification and intervention, fostering research, and protecting their rights under the law. LDA seeks to accomplish this through awareness, advocacy, empowerment, education, service and collaborative efforts."

LD ONLINE

Internet: www.ldonline.org

According to their website, LD onLine

"offers a vast array of information on topics within the area of learning disabilities. Here you'll find articles written by the leading experts, research findings reported by top researchers, and the latest news in the field of learning disabilities."

NATIONAL CENTER FOR LEARNING DISABILITIES (NCLD)

Headquarters: 381 Park Avenue South, Suite 1401,
New York NY 10016
Telephone: 888-575-7373; 212-545-7510
Internet: www.ncld.org

NCLD "provides national leadership in support of children and adults with learning disabilities (LD) by offering information, resources, and referral services; developing and supporting innovative educational programs; promoting public awareness; and advocating for more effective policies and legislation to help individuals with learning disabilities." Its mission is

"to increase opportunities for all individuals with learning disabilities to achieve their potential. NCLD accomplishes its mission by increasing public awareness and understanding of learning disabilities, conducting educational programs and services that promote research-based knowledge, and providing national leadership in shaping public policy. We provide solutions that help people with LD participate fully in society."

NATIONAL CENTER ON ADDICTION AND SUBSTANCE ABUSE (CASA)

Headquarters: Columbia University, 613 Third Avenue,
19th Floor, New York, NY 10017-6706
Telephone: 212-841-5200
Internet: casacolumbia.org

CASA's main concern is substance abuse, but because many people being treated for substance abuse have learning disabilities, CASA has promoted research in the relationship between learning disabilities and substance abuse.

NATIONAL INSTITUTE FOR LITERACY (NIFL)

Headquarters: 1775 I Street, NW, Suite 730,
             Washington, DC 20006-2401
Telephone: 202-233-2025
Internet: nifl.gov

The National Institute for Literacy, created by the 1991 National Literacy Act, is "an independent federal organization leading the national effort toward a fully literate nation in the 21st century." Its goal is

> "to ensure that all Americans with literacy needs have access to services that can help them gain the basic skills necessary for success in the workplace, family, and community in the 21st century."

The institute helps coordinate public and private activities promoting literacy services on the regional, state and federal levels. A specific goal is to improve services for adults with learning disabilities.

NATIONAL INSTITUTES FOR HEALTH (NIH)

Headquarters: 9000 Rockville Pike
             Bethesda, MD 20892
Telephone: 301-496-4000
Internet: www.nih.gov

Although learning disabilities are by no means its primary focus, NIH sponsors enough research on learning disabilities and related issues to make it a useful resource. The National Institute of Mental Health (NIMH), the National Institute of Neurological Disorders and Strokes (NIND) and the National Institute of Child Health and Human Development (NICHD) are especially useful.

SCHWAB LEARNING CENTER

Headquarters: 1650 South Amphlett Boulevard, Suite 300
San Mateo, CA 94402
Internet: www.schwablearning.org

Schwab Learning Center is a nonprofit, child-focused organization that has "been providing LD information and resources to parents since 1988." Its vision is "to help kids with learning differences be successful in learning and life." The web site information continues:

"We've conducted studies to understand how LD impacts the child, the parent and the family. We've combined our experience with our findings in this Web site in order to help parents become agents of success in their children's lives."

SMART KIDS WITH LEARNING DISABILITIES, INC.

Headquarters: P. O. Box 2726
Westport, CT 06880
Internet: www.SmartKidswithLD.org

This organization puts out a bimonthly newsletter called *Smart Kids* and has a very informative website. Its statement of purpose says:

"As a non-profit organization, we are dedicated to providing parents (and teachers) of children with learning issues with current information from leading professionals, along with practical advice and encouragement. **Smart Kids** also works to increase public awareness of our children's strengths, as well as their difficulties."

U. S. DEPARTMENT OF JUSTICE

Headquarters: 950 Pennsylvania Ave., NW
Washington, DC 20530

The U. S. Department of Justice is responsible for administering the Americans with Disabilities Act. The department has an ADA Home Page, accessed at

www.usdoj.gov/crt/ada/adahom1.htm

The toll-free ADA Information Line is 1-800-514-0301 (voice) or

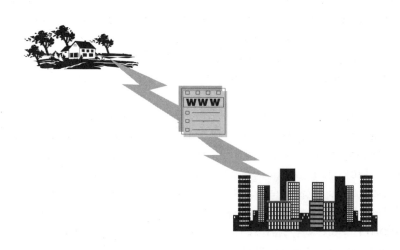

Appendix

Social Costs of Learning Disabilities

The relationship between learning disabilities and social and emotional problems seems too obvious to need explaining, to those of us who have lived with both. In Arlyn J. Roffman's book, *Meeting the Challenge of Learning Disabilities in Adulthood* (Paul H. Brookes Publishing Co., 2000), the author lists some of the effects of learning disabilities on adults' mental health. These secondary effects are sometimes called the "emotional overlay," she says. They include irritability and mood swings, low self-esteem, depression, stress and anxiety, and substance abuse.

The causal relationship between learning disabilities and bad temper can be explained in several ways, Roffman writes. For one thing, one characteristic of learning disabilities is impulsivity, or lack of inhibitions, or inability to think before speaking or acting; thus, an angry impulse is promptly expressed. Also, adults with learning disabilities functioning in a world where the majority neither shares nor understands their problems are frequently frustrated and overwhelmed and, like people without learning disabilities, get short-tempered as a consequence. Third, many adults whose disabilities went undiagnosed until they had repeatedly failed in school and at work feel cheated and angry. And finally, Roffman suggests, people with learning disabilities may hide their unhappiness and insecurity by acting angry and defiant.

Roffman emphasizes other consequences of learning disabilities for adults. For example, she has several chapters on the effects of learning disabilities on relationships, including friendships, romances and parent-child relations. Some are obvious: People with dygraphia cannot write affectionate notes to their spouses; people with dyslexia cannot read bedtime stories to their children. Others are more subtle. For example, many people with learning disabilities either lack tactile sense, or are disproportionately affected by a touch. Someone with the first form of disability cannot easily shake hands; the grip may be painfully firm, or uncomfortably weak. An overreaction to tactile stimulation means casual touching is unwelcome, a difficult thing to explain to a parent, spouse, or child.

People with learning disabilities often lack social skills, Roffman points out. Depending on the form of disability, they may have trouble remembering names and faces and therefore not recognize people they should know; they may be unobservant about dress, body language, and other signals that help people fit in; they may lack the concept of "personal distance" and make others uncomfortable by getting too close or staying too distant.

Because people with learning disabilities graduate from or quit high school without being taught the basic skills we need to earn a living, it is difficult for many of us to get and keep a job. Even those of us fortunate enough to find and use our talent, whether it's boat building or trumpet playing, are sometimes so overwhelmed by our emotional baggage that we cannot function. At the LDA International Conference in February 2001, Ron Hume, President of the Learning Disabilities Association of Washington State, cited a study which found that 62% of students with learning disabilities were unemployed a year after graduating from high school — and those are the students who managed to graduate. Over half of the people receiving unemployment benefits have learning disabilities. There again, we comprise only 10% of the population, so our incidence is much, much higher.

Another area we've become aware of in the last few years is that, of all the people that are receiving welfare of any kind, over half of them have learning disabilities. An August 2000 Fact Sheet from LDA reported a 1997 Washington State study which found that 54% of those on welfare had a learning disability. A 1992 report from the Office of the Inspector General that Ron Hume cited said that the two most common reasons welfare clients could not get or keep a job were substance abuse and learning disabilities. Fact sheets prepared by the National Institute for Literacy (NIFL) indicate that the average young adult welfare recipient is reading at a sixth-grade level, and that the fewer the educational skills, the longer a client stays on welfare, on average.

Difficulties with reading, writing, and computation are not the only effects of learning disabilities. A NIFL Fact Sheet on "literacy and learning disabilities" pointed out that the types of troubles caused by learning disabilities include organizational, planning, and scheduling problems (that is, a lack of executive function abilities), inability to remain attentive long enough to complete tasks, and inadequate social skills to get along with co-workers.

NIFL also found a link between literacy and income. For example, welfare recipients with low literacy skills work an average of 11 weeks a year, while those who are more literate work an average of 29 weeks. 43% percent of adults with low literacy skills live in poverty, NIFL found, compared to fewer than 5% of adults who can read and write at an age-appropriate level. The government is trying very hard to get people off the welfare rolls and back being self-sufficient and independent and having a job. They are beginning to address some of the needs to help these folks.

Another area that is extremely high, and we don't have good statistics on it, but learning disabilities are very high among the homeless; probably well over 50%. I try to be careful about statistics, because some of the studies don't cover exactly the same population that other studies do. Sometimes I feel that I'm out ahead of the statistics, or out ahead of the studies, working without any real research to back up some of the things that I'm saying. There's no question in my mind, however, that millions of people out there are failing, and it is their difficulties in either language or math that have led to other kinds of failures, also. When you consider what is happening, I think it points out that we need to do a lot of things that we have already started. This is in the area of early identification and early intervention. We now know how to educate people with disabilities, and it will lead to education without the failure that we're experiencing now.

As discussed above, people with learning disabilities are disproportionately represented in the correctional system. Carolyn Eggleston, Ph.D., developed three theories to explain the correlation between learning disabilities and youth crime. She calls them the "susceptibility theory," the "school failure theory," and the "different treatment" theory. As summarized in Ron Hume's February 2001 presentation to the LDA conference, the "susceptibility theory" holds that, because young people with learning disabilities are apt to be impulsive, easily led, and insensitive to other people's motives and to the consequences of their actions, it is easy to get them into trouble. The "school failure theory" holds that youngsters react to repeated academic and social failure by seeking acceptance in other, less socially desirable ways. And the "different treatment" theory holds that, once in the hands of the police, youngsters with learning disabilities react in inappropriate ways, which earn them harsher treatment.

Hume supported Eggleston's third theory with information from a March 1997 focus group, sponsored by the U. S. Department of Education and others, on the fate of young people with disabilities in the juvenile justice system. Key conclusions Hume cited were:

- the juvenile justice system and the individual professionals who deal with young offenders seldom understand the special needs and characteristics of people with learning disabilities; and

- once in the system, youngsters with learning disabilities seldom behave well enough to shorten their jail terms, and often become repeat offenders.

NIFL has similarly concluded that people in prison generally are significantly less literate than the general population, and that education helps an ex-prisoner stay out. A NIFL Fact Sheet says that only 51% of prisoners have a high school diploma or equivalent, compared to 76% of the general population. Although the federal prison system has been requiring literacy training since 1982, NIFL estimated that no more than 10% of prisoners who need literacy education actually get it. For those who do improve their literacy, preliminary studies show benefits. NIFL cites a Virginia study of 3,000 inmates which found that 49% of those who did not join prison educational programs ended up back in prison, while only 20% of prisoners who did improve their education were re-arrested.

As I previously reported, I think 50% of the young adults in substance abuse have learning disabilities; probably 70% of the older adults do. I have seen one study that put the incidence at 60%. So, even though my numbers are anecdotal, I feel that they are quite close.

In the 1980s, very little was known about a correlation between learning disabilities and substance abuse. There were probably other cooperative ventures like the one I've described, but they were isolated. There was no national program to study what some of us were finding to be true — that many people who abuse drugs or alcohol have a learning disability. Because so little attention was being paid to the possibility of a connection, there were no scientific efforts to understand it.

On Feb. 1, 1999, the situation changed. That was the date of a conference on the relationship between learning disabilities and substance abuse, sponsored jointly by The National Center on Addiction and Substance Abuse at Columbia University (known as CASA) and the National Center for Learning Disabilities (NCLD). The conference brought together experts from both fields, substance abuse and learning disabilities (including Dr. Larry Silver, who in 2000 was elected president of the Learning Disabilities Association of America). In September 2000, CASA published a white paper titled "Substance Abuse and Learning Disabilities: Peas in a Pod or Apples and Oranges?"

According to information from CASA's web site, there is clear evidence of correlations among substance abuse, learning disabilities, and behavioral disorders (such as ADD and ADHD). However, there is not yet evidence of any causal relationship in either direction; that is, no evidence that any one of these three problems causes any of the others. CASA reports that a child with learning disabilities is twice as likely also to have ADD than is a child without learning disabilities. There is a strong correlation between ADD and substance abuse; CASA reports that many substance abusers have ADD, and perhaps half of all people with ADD overuse alcohol or drugs.

Perhaps most important, the CASA report points out that the young people most likely to turn to drugs or alcohol or both are those who do not fit in socially with their peers. These are the youngsters who are taunted for doing poorly in class or for their clumsiness on the sports field, and who therefore feel isolated and rejected. As we have seen, the student with learning disabilities often falls into this group. CASA recommends early identification and treatment of learning disabilities as one way to prevent substance abuse later in life. Its report further advises that when a youngster in counseling for substance abuse also has learning disabilities, effective treatment must address both problems.

On Jan. 31, 2000, CASA released a second report, called "Shoveling Up: The Impact of Substance Abuse on State Budgets." Based on surveys of all 50 states (estimates were made for the five that did not reply) plus the District of Columbia and Puerto Rico, the report put the 1998 cost to states of substance abuse and addiction at $81.3 billion. That figure does not include federal government, local government, school, or private costs; nor does the report attempt to quantify the human suffering that substance abuse causes to the abusers, their family and friends, and their victims. The CASA report said that the $81.3 billion represented 13.1% of total state spending in 1998. The spending was divided among states' justice systems (it represented, on average, 77% of total justice spending), education allocations, health costs, child and family assistance programs, mental health and developmental disabilities programs, and public safety.

The CASA report further stated that, on average, 96% of the states' substance abuse spending was used to "shovel up the wreckage" (deal with drug-related crime, and pay welfare costs, for example) and only 4% went for prevention and treatment programs. On average again, every taxpayer paid $277 in annual state taxes to "shovel up" and $10 a year to prevent or treat substance abuse, the report said. The report recommended that state officials reverse that emphasis, devoting more effort and money to prevention and treatment. Based on CASA's earlier findings, diagnosing and treating learning disabilities might well be part of a prevention program.

Everything we know and are finding out points to the plain fact that, if people with learning disabilities are educated in ways that make sense *to them*, they will be happier and more productive and will be a lot less likely to become part of the costly "wreckage." It makes good sense to redirect some of our resources toward doing that; it makes no sense not to.